ALSO BY HELEN EPSTEIN

Children of the Holocaust

Where She Came From

Joe Papp: An American Life

Music Talks

Tina Packer Builds a Theater

Looking Back: Memoir of a Psychoanalyst
(with Paul Ornstein)

Under A Cruel Star by Heda Kovály
(translation)

Archivist on a Bicycle

Écrire la vie

The Long Half-Lives of Love and Trauma

Helen Epstein

Plunkett Lake Press

Praise for *The Long Half-Lives of Love and Trauma*

"In this poignant, vividly written and fearlessly frank memoir, Helen Epstein delves into her own and her family's difficult past, and probes, with sensitivity and insight, the multi-layered ambiguities of love, intimate relationships, and post-Holocaust American lives. More than a chronicle of events, this is a true labor of memory, in which the story of the body is inseparable from the narrative of the self."
— **Eva Hoffman**, author of *Lost in Translation*

"Helen Epstein has crafted an unclassifiable masterwork of nonfiction from the materials of personal memory, family history, romance, and trauma. Never in her distinguished career has Epstein written more openly or more beautifully." — **David Hajdu,** author of *Positively 4th Street: The Lives and Times of Joan Baez, Bob Dylan, Mimi Baez Fariña, and Richard Fariña*

"This book invents its own genre. Eminent journalist Helen Epstein suspects sexual abuse in her childhood and investigates with the full arsenal of what is available to her as an adult: the literature on trauma and false memory; the tools of psychoanalysis as well as a sophisticated understanding of its limitations; the toolkits of an historian and ethnographer. And access to a key witness... That rare story in which everyone becomes more human and multi-dimensional as it unfolds."
— **Sherry Turkle**, author of *Reclaiming Conversation: The Power of Talk in a Digital Age*

"In midlife, well settled in marriage and motherhood, Epstein is impelled to revisit the legacy of her childhood. As she risks both her own sanity and the relationships she holds most dear, Epstein illustrates the complex moral and psychological effects of trauma, and the gritty process of recovery." — **Judith Herman, M.D.**, author of *Trauma and Recovery*

"Helen Epstein's career has been devoted to tracking how political and cultural history penetrates family life over generations. Her books have been models of investigation. This new memoir plants an even deeper stake into the search through personal trauma, seeking over long, harrowing years, the sibylline voice of truth. This is heroic writing, and belongs in the canon of accounts of mothers and daughters, of wounds lost in the depth of childhood, and the valiant determination of a woman to live in uncertainty with grace." — **Patricia Hampl**, author of *I Could Tell You Stories*

"In this riveting book, Helen Epstein probes the dark corners of her childhood with sensitivity and remarkable candor. This memoir reads like a detective story and asks questions that affect us all: how does our sexual nature get formed or deformed, and how can it change? Unflinching writing." — **Anne Karpf**, author of *The War After: Living with the Holocaust*

"Courageously peeling back layers of her own psyche, Helen Epstein describes how one is able to withstand and survive trauma, and – perhaps even more difficult – to heal from it. While tracing her own trajectory, Epstein offers a riveting cultural history of America in the late twentieth century." — **Helen Fremont**, author of *After Long Silence*

"A fascinating exploration of the mechanisms of memory, with the author's first love and her psychoanalyst as witnesses. Step by step Epstein leads us on a brave voyage into the recognition of the healing power of understanding and forgiving." — **Savyon Liebrecht**, author of *Apples from the Desert* and *A Good Place for the Night*

"Helen Epstein has given us a fascinating and unique literary gift. This book takes us on a deeply insightful retrospective journey: from a 21st century suburb of New England, back through the second world war, through the dark secrets of refugee New York City in the 1950s, through a psychoanalysis with a flexible but disciplined analyst. A must-read for anyone interested in life, love, trauma, and the human condition." — **Ira Brenner M.D.**, author of *Dark Matters: Exploring the Realm of Psychic Trauma*

"I couldn't put it down. Once again master storyteller and journalist Helen Epstein blazes new trails with this mashup of memoir, historical and journalistic research, and science. The world of survivors she vividly re-creates is both historically revealing and relevant for today. In this rare opportunity for a do-over, you will find yourself asking questions about memory and marriage, family and forgiveness, trauma and truth." — **Faith Adiele**, author of *Meeting Faith: An Inward Odyssey*

"In her courage and willingness to be vulnerable, Helen Epstein demonstrates what it means to come home to oneself. This is a revelatory exploration of integration — inviting the fractures of the past to be seen clearly enough that they can inform, but no longer define who we are. Those of us who seek such integration can learn much from Epstein's clear, thoughtful writing and her fearless examination of a murky, dramatic, wrenching past." — **Maria Sirois**, author of *A Short Course in Happiness After Loss (and Other Dark, Difficult Times)*

Cover design by Becky Hunt and Susan Erony (susanerony.com)

Library of Congress Cataloging-in-Publication Data

Names: Epstein, Helen, 1947- author.
Title: The long half-lives of love and trauma / by Helen Epstein.
Description: First edition. | Lexington, Massachusetts : Plunkett Lake Press, 2018.
Identifiers: LCCN 2017035710 | ISBN 0961469665 (pbk.)
Subjects: LCSH: Epstein, Helen, 1947- | Children of Holocaust survivors--New York (State)--New York--Biography. | First loves--United States.
Classification: LCC D804.3 E675 2018 | DDC 818/.5403 [B] --dc23
LC record available at https://lccn.loc.gov/2017035710

"Killing the angel in the house I think I solved. She died. But telling the truth about my own experience as a body, I do not think I solved. I doubt that any woman has solved it yet. The obstacles against her are still immensely powerful — and yet they are very difficult to define. Outwardly, what is simpler than to write books? Inwardly, I think, the case is very different; she still has many ghosts to fight, many prejudices to overcome."

— Virginia Woolf, 1931

"Le travail de la mémoire peut être un travail dangereux, à ne pas accomplir en solitaire."

— Régine Waintrater, 2001

Author's Note

The Long Half-Lives of Love and Trauma is a work of non-fiction, but some names and places have been changed to protect privacy.

~ 1 ~

We moved for the schools. Our town was just eight miles from the city, but it felt like another world with its white clapboard houses and churches, acres of school baseball, football, and soccer fields; its swimming pools and year-round ice-skating rink. All of it looked unreal to me, and suspiciously safe. I was 52. I had grown up in New York City and had always thought of the suburbs as a form of death.

My urban habits didn't transfer: no more walking to bookstores and museums; no more window-shopping or people-watching. There were few sidewalks and almost no pedestrians. I missed street life, distraction, even the subtle drumbeat of danger.

Conversation in this new place trended toward two subjects: children and real estate. I learned new words like "tear-down" and "McMansion." I was asked whether we would be employing a service. A service? Everywhere I looked those first weeks, crews of uniformed men were editing the landscape, taking out bushes, installing trees, spraying on lawns with hosefuls of lurid hydro-seed.

My new surroundings had no soundtrack. I rarely heard a honk or a siren. Our street was so silent that, for what seemed the first time, I could listen for what was going on inside me.

Our kids said our new house felt lonely and I thought so too. Even my husband Patrick thought there was too much space, within our new rooms and between them. I'd get lost driving back and forth from the Stop and Shop. A few times I drove past my own house.

I was driving down yet another picturesque street when Robbie's voice came sailing from the radio, sounding as though we'd been talking just minutes before.

"I suppose all teenagers have some secret they hide from their parents," he was saying. "For me, it wasn't a copy of *Playboy* or a pack of cigarettes. No, my hidden treasure was..."

It was late afternoon. I had groceries in the van, food that needed refrigeration, but I pulled over to the side of the road.

There's no mistaking the voice of your first love. Robbie's was husky, conspiratorial and a little wry, as though he knew I was sitting in my minivan in an upscale suburb listening to him. I listened not just to his words, but to the sound of his voice. It soothed me. It said: some things don't change. This is who I am, still who I once was.

~ 2 ~

A few days later, I received an invitation to speak at a college in California not far from where Robbie now lived. I had published *Children of the Holocaust,* a book about sons and daughters of survivors, some 20 years before and had been lecturing on the effects of trauma on a second generation of people ever since. Robbie was second generation too, a son not of Holocaust survivors but of blacklisted American Communists. I had fallen in love with him when I was a teenager and never entirely fell out.

We all carry cameos in our minds: miniature, idealized portraits of those who most deeply touched our lives. Apart from my parents, I carried no portrait more vivid than Robbie's. I'd had several more intimate friends. I'd lived with men whose bodies I came to know far better than I ever knew his. I had married, given birth, raised two sons with my husband. But throughout it all, like some endlessly looping song, Robbie's voice and face remained embedded in my being.

What was he exactly? Not a crush or even an authentic boyfriend, but a conflation of caring guides: my chaperone, my teacher, my eventual lover. Robbie had also been my model of the artist I wished to become. From the start, he had been a kind of ghost, appearing at key moments in my life and then disappearing — for over three decades.

I was 15 when we met at our piano teacher's studio. "Fresh as a peach," my mother embarrassed me by saying. I didn't like to be compared to fruit or, as my father said, also in Czech, "a tadpole." I had always been one of the taller girls in my classes but after puberty I grew to nearly six feet — an uncommon height for a girl in 1963. My breasts grew too, from ironing board flat to what girls called "developed" and boys called "stacked."

I did what I could to make myself inconspicuous. Where there was a wall or table, I leaned on it. I wore flat-heeled shoes and loose sweaters. I walked quickly, shoulders hunched forward, as if I were hurrying in from the rain.

Maybe if I'd been born in the twenty-first century, I might have seen my body as a source of power. I had friends who did, while I wished I could be invisible. I still sometimes do. When women friends complain about men's eyes passing over them and moving on, I think: what a relief!

My piano teacher was one of the few men back then who seemed oblivious to my body. For Mr. Labovitz, everything was about the music. I didn't know about his role in Manhattan's left-wing community. I wouldn't have known then what "left-wing" meant. He was my piano teacher; that was all I thought.

"What did you prepare?" Mr. Labovitz asked when I arrived.

It didn't matter. I knew I wasn't born to be a musician and Mr. Labovitz knew it too. But my mother insisted that I learn piano, he had to make a living and, at least, I liked music.

When I was seven, Franci bought an old upright and set aside half an hour a day to cajole me into practicing. She bought the appropriate books; she applied herself to my instruction with the concentration she applied to making clothes. But even if she hadn't been tense from a day of managing customers and employees in her *salon,* my mother had no idea of how to teach. We would argue about which Easy Duet to play, I would complain that my part was too hard or boring, that I was tired or that she was playing too fast. In the end, I would flounce off and leave my mother on the piano bench alone, improvising jazz standards from the 1930s.

One day, I said if she didn't find a real teacher, I would never touch a piano again, and she found Mr. Labovitz. She gave up the fantasy of my becoming a famous pianist but not her desire that I learn the repertoire she had learned as a girl: Bach, Mozart, Beethoven and Chopin. They were, to her, my inheritance: part of the cultural capital of every well-brought-up European girl since the invention of its middle class.

Every six months, Mr. Labovitz held a recital in which his students performed for one another. He expected us to dress for the occasion and I wore an outfit from my mother's *salon.* She made elegant, well-constructed clothes that a woman had to fit into rather than the other way around and I felt taller and more awkward than usual. I knew none of the other piano students and was relieved when Mr. Labovitz stood between the two grand pianos and asked everyone to find a seat.

"Hi Robbie," he waved to a boy who came in just before the first student began to play. "Have a seat."

The recital proceeded uneventfully. When it was my turn I went to the piano and when I finished, there was the requisite applause. I had made no major mistakes. But I was aware that every time I learned a piece of music, Mr. Labovitz had to show me how to play it, as though he were translating from a foreign language. Only rarely could I play what the composer intended the way that I could read a book and know what the author meant. After I returned to my seat, he said, "Robbie?"

The boy who came in late sat down at the piano. He rolled up the sleeves of his white shirt to the elbows. I noticed that his pants were rumpled, his hair uncombed. He leaned over the keyboard and seemed to be waiting for something. Then he dove into the music. The piano I had played sounded like a different instrument. It was evident that piano lessons were something that he loved. I was sure Mr. Labovitz never had to exhort him, as he did me, to "play with conviction!"

My mother worshipped men who played the piano. My father fell asleep at concerts, so from the time I was four or five, I was her date. We climbed the stairs together to the top rung of Carnegie Hall. My mother always bought tickets on the keyboard side so that through her opera glasses we could watch the pianist's hands — as though by watching, you might learn to make magic.

For Franci, a concert hall was asylum, spa, and spiritual retreat in one. Taking me with her was a re-enactment of a ritual she had performed with her mother, before she lost her. For me, a concert hall was the rare place where I had my mother at least partly to myself.

She sat rapt at the edge of her seat, opera glasses to her face, while I zoned in and out of the music. When it was lively, I paid attention. When it was slow, I turned my mind to the pastry tray in the downstairs café. At intermission, before we left our seats, my mother opened her purse and took out her silver lipstick holder. She swiveled the red stick out of its container, and painted her lips bright red. Then we went downstairs to the café. While my mother and her friends smoked, I would gobble down an éclair or napoleon.

That Sunday afternoon when Robbie played, I paid attention to the music. He made the notes sound like words and, although I could not have said what those words actually meant, they spoke to me. It was over before I was ready. People stood up. Mrs. Labovitz asked me to help her in the kitchen. When I came back out, Robbie was gone.

~ 3 ~

For 30 years, even when we lived on different continents, Robbie and I kept in touch. He read what I published; I listened to what he composed and, later, to what he said on the radio. Every now and then, Robbie would propose that we collaborate on a project but I always found reasons to refuse. We weren't a good fit. I liked clear objectives and deadlines; he liked chasing amorphous subjects. Most important, I thought I'd wind up as scribe to the genius.

But when I received my invitation to speak in California in the fall of 1999, I thought we might work together on a book. I had been thinking about first love, my atypical adolescence and how the massive trauma of the Holocaust had affected survivors and their children in the intimate realms of sex and friendship — a theme that I had not been able to delve into in my first book. But, almost as soon as I began thinking about myself as a teenage girl, I ran into gaps and great patches of murk.

Robbie, I reflected, was a reliable source. He had come to our home for dinner every week after we first met, was fascinated by my parents, and continued to visit throughout my adolescence. He had known my two younger brothers and most of my friends. He could validate what I remembered, and remember what I'd forgotten. He could serve as my archive, mirror and muse.

I questioned those words as soon as I thought them. Why would I need an archive to write a memoir? Wasn't my own memory sufficient? And what made me think that Robbie would help? We hadn't seen one another in a dozen years.

Robbie sounded unsurprised to hear from me, as though we were picking up a conversation interrupted a few days instead of a few years before.

When I told him I had been invited to speak at a college near his home, he said, "Come." When I asked if he'd be interested in helping me research a book, he said, "Sure."

I was relieved, then alarmed. Why was he agreeing so quickly? Boredom? Middle-age, with its autumnal mix of panic and regret? Was he also feeling a need to reconnect with his early life?

I knew better than to ask. Robbie often responded to questions as though they were provocations. Unlike my marriage to Patrick — late, stable, a broad band of shared experience — my relationship with Robbie was like a narrow radio frequency, subject to static and frequent loss of signal. It was something of a mystery why our connection had lasted as long as it had.

We agreed that I would spend time with him when I spoke in California and that, meanwhile, I would email him pieces of what I was writing. He would give me feedback.

~ 4 ~

I began to write about the recital where I first saw Robbie, after which my piano teacher asked me if I liked to sing.

I thought that was a dumb question. Even my tone-deaf father liked to sing. I sang Beatles and civil rights songs with my friends and lullabies to my baby brother. I could have said that I knew every song in every musical then playing on Broadway, that I wanted to be a musical comedy star, and that I had even chosen a stage name — Carol Brent — and dropped it only after my mother let me know it was a brand of socks. But all I said was "Yeah."

"Well, stand up!" said Mr. Labovitz. "Sing something!"

I remembered an art song we were taught in school: *"Ah, Sweet Mystery of Life, At Last I've Found You! Ah, At Last I Know the Secret of It All!"*

Mr. Labovitz stopped me before the lyrics revealed that the secret was love. Then he said that if I promised to be on time, I could become a member of his chorus on the following Monday night. "You can tell your parents I'll see to it that you get home safely."

When I arrived, I found my piano teacher alone, setting up metal folding chairs in a semi-circle around the piano. He handed me a chair and said, in his brusque way, that Robbie Ross would be driving me home.

The boy who played Bach was going to drive me home? I kept my trench coat on as Mr. Labovitz introduced me to the accompanist, a few singers, and an oily-faced teenage boy who had also played at the recital. At seven-thirty, Mr. Labovitz handed out scores and said it was time to start.

He didn't seem embarrassed that there were twice as many empty chairs as singers. I realized that I was the entire alto section and sank deeper into my trench coat. Then Mr. Labovitz raised his right arm, the accompanist began playing, and we were off like a train on a track of sound, and I was scrambling to keep up.

Every once in a while, he shouted "Letter B" or "One after C," reassuring me that I was in the right place. I was so afraid I would miss a beat and produce a sound when the score called for silence that I began to whimper instead of singing out and my teacher, conducting energetically, bored his eyes into mine and shouted, "Where are the Altos?"

I wondered where they were too. I wondered whether Robbie would come and if he didn't, who would take me home. I wondered whether this was a typical night for the chorus or whether lots of singers were sick. Fifteen minutes into rehearsal the door opened and Robbie came in, carrying a large black guitar case. He set it down and said, "Sorry."

"Will you sing Alto please?" Mr. Labovitz handed him a score and gestured to the chair next to mine.

Robbie sang as easily as he had played the piano. I followed him, a fraction of a second later, but fast enough so that it sounded like there actually was an alto section. When Mr. Labovitz suddenly said, "Let's take five minutes," I felt like a fish thrown up out of the ocean and onto the beach.

The chorus members stood up to stretch and talk. Nobody paid attention to me and I decided it was safe to take off my coat. I watched Robbie walk over to Mr. Labovitz, put his hand on his shoulder and — this was a shock — call him "Dave." I watched him joke with the oily-faced boy. They jabbed and poked each other, trading sick jokes. "What does a Helen Keller doll do when you wind her up?" "How did the paraplegic brush his teeth?"

I thought they were disgusting.

Mr. Labovitz called for order and we were off again until ten when he stopped conducting. Robbie leaned over my chair and asked, "Where do you live?"

I opened my mouth and my address came out in a squeak.

We walked through the dark streets to his car. He stopped at an old Chevy and when he unlocked the door, I saw a history of doughnuts, potato chip bags, old coffee cups, book covers, crumpled newspapers. Robbie threw what was on the front seat to the back seat, threw his jacket over it, and placed his guitar case on top of that.

I felt as though I had died and come back as Nancy Drew, my girls' books heroine. Nancy lived in the Midwest and had a boyfriend named Ned who drove her to dams and drive-ins where they would park and kiss. Robbie swung his right hand over the back of my seat like Ned, looked over his shoulder, and slowly backed up. Then he swung his arm back to the wheel and drove me home. He told me he was a scholarship student at college and gave guitar lessons to children to pay his expenses. He said he was 18, three years older than me.

I sat still as a deer. I knew few boys, few American boys, no American boys who went to college. "You were silent and I was fascinated," Robbie told me much later. "I thought it aloofness and mystery. I imagined all sorts of things."

Decades later, I still remember his arm behind my neck like a flame, and myself staring through the windshield into the dark.

~ 5 ~

In the fall of 1963 when I met Robbie, we lived at 170 West 73rd St, in a large apartment building overlooking a square dubbed Needle Park. Our Manhattan neighborhood was dangerous by the standards of that time, home to bums, junkies and the teen-age gangs dramatized in *West Side Story.*

Some of my mother's adventuresome customers enjoyed a thrill when their chauffeurs pulled up at a curb frequented by winos, transvestites, and drug dealers. Others complained about how long it took to get a taxi. The most calculating tried to whittle down my mother's prices: her *salon* was on Amsterdam not Madison Avenue. There was no elevator man, no doorman, and all that graffiti scratched into the walls of the elevator.

But my mother was a European *couturière* who had studied in Berlin and Paris. The dowdy Eisenhower years had given way to the New Frontier; Jacqueline Kennedy was into *haute couture* and women everywhere were trying to emulate her style. My mother could help them. Dark-eyed, dark-haired, she worked with a cigarette dangling from her lips and a tape measure around her neck like Coco Chanel, and spoke with an accent that was continental if not French. Her authority reassured clients and persuaded them to overlook the fact that Frances Epstein, Inc. — as my mother named her *salon* in New York — was located on the wrong side of town.

It would have been better for business, my mother said, if we lived on the East Side, but landlords there didn't rent to Jews.

Besides, the most interesting writers and artists lived on the West Side, where in 1963 you could still find a pre-war, rent-controlled, seven-room apartment like ours for $200 a month. Poor Puerto Rican and Irish families lived in brownstones on the side streets. Rich people lived on Riverside Drive and Central Park West, in stately buildings with names instead of numbers — The Majestic, The San Remo, The Dakota.

Some of my classmates lived in those buildings and, after school, I took note of the uniformed doormen, elevator men, maids, and master bedrooms where American parents slept. What should have been the master bedroom of our own apartment was my mother's workroom with its sewing machines, headless mannequins, irons, and my mother's cutting table with its chalks, spools of thread, scissors and pinking shears.

What should have been our living room was what my mother called the *salon.* She held fittings near the windows, before a floor-to-ceiling, three-way mirror. There, standing on a revolving circular platform, customers gazed at their triple reflections while my mother knelt to pin hems and seams. At the other end, in a carpeted sitting area, they sat on my parents' beds, disguised by bolsters and pillows to form a couch-like L around a glass coffee table.

During the day, the table was piled with books of fabric samples, *Vogue, Bazaar,* and *L'Officiel* that customers perused as they smoked. Every night, my parents moved it away and went to sleep.

Fur coats often lay across the bolsters when I came home from school and expensive jewelry on the glass table, so that a bracelet or ring would not tear fragile fabric during a fitting. My two younger brothers were banned from the *salon* but I was allowed in. Often a half-naked customer in a lacy slip held out her arms to embrace me and I inhaled the scent of face cream and cigarette smoke mixed with perfume: the scent I came to associate with what lay ahead in my life as a woman.

I was both fascinated by and jealous of the customers, their bodies, their stories, and the attention they received from my mother. She was patient with them, no matter how they behaved. She had her favorites: painter Lily Harmon, who was "a dream to dress" and was married to a rich man; Mrs. Hoover, who was on the board of the Metropolitan Opera Guild and ordered everything in navy blue; actress Vivian Vance from the *I Love Lucy* show who was plump but never difficult.

I knew to disappear when a Mrs. Sinatra or Mrs. Albee or, later, Mrs. Trump was having a fitting. Women attached to famous men, my mother said, could cause more trouble than their connections were worth. In the 1950s, one of the Mrs. Lerners had absconded to the Yucatán with her clothes, bill unpaid. "I wouldn't want to share a prison cell with any of these dames," Franci said. Prison was one of her usual frames of reference.

My mother's mood depended on who came to the *salon* and I was always relieved when it was Mrs. Lewis. She ordered evening gowns, dresses, suits and coats, for herself and her sister. Born into a poor family in Texas, Hester Lewis became a Hollywood starlet and married a man whose company made most of the spark plugs in American cars.

"Isn't this beautiful?" she would murmur as my mother held out a glamorous creation like the silk chiffon lounging outfit that had paid our rent for four months.

"Beautiful on you," my mother would mutter, careful not to drop cigarette ash on Mrs. Lewis. Then, using the Czech endearment, "*Kočičko,* make us some tea."

My mother called me "Pussycat" when she was relaxed, and Mrs. Lewis was one of the very few people who relaxed her. She was never finicky or in a hurry. She didn't seem to work, even at being beautiful. Her only job, as I understood it then, was to accompany her husband as he flew between their homes in Ohio and Florida and Virginia. She didn't go to the opera or read books. She had never been to Europe and — to my mother's dismay — didn't care. Her idea of a good time was to shop for people she liked, including me. She also liked to ask me about boys.

I had told her that when I was eleven, I had had a boyfriend, but since graduating to an all-girls' school, none.

"She has a very rich cousin who's in love with her," my mother, who enjoyed this kind of conversation, would say. "He's 16 years older and just waiting for her to grow up."

"Do you like him?" Mrs. Lewis would ask, and when I shook my head say, "You might change your mind. You can marry more money in five minutes than you can make in fifty years."

My mother didn't contradict her. In *koncentrák* too, she often said, beautiful women had also leveraged their looks for food — for themselves and their mothers. On the other hand, some beautiful women had wound up murdered or raped. You needed brains too.

I hated it when my mother dropped the word "concentration camp" into conversation, like ash from her cigarettes. It disturbed me even more than the line of blue inked numbers visible on her forearm. The Auschwitz tattoo was a constant reminder to her customers that their gifted *couturière* was also a canny survivor. Franci had told some of them the story: during a selection, she had claimed to be an electrician, not a dressmaker and lying had saved her life.

Unlike the George Washington I learned about at school, she didn't hesitate to lie when necessary. When I entered grade school and we lived just outside the district, Franci registered me as living at her business partner's apartment in the Dakota. In the *salon,* too, I sensed that much of her time was spent in deception: not only in the usual business of selling things to reluctant customers but in hiding or disguising their flaws and exaggerating or creating new assets. She padded breasts, shoulders and *derrières.* She even made short stocky Mrs. Korner, who was shaped like an inverted V, look normal.

My mother brought an unsentimental pragmatism to her work as well as to the anecdotes from the *salon* that she told me. Mrs. Lewis and Lily had done well to marry rich. Romance was for Hollywood. Poverty was hard. My great-grandmother had been so poor she had jumped from a window in Vienna. My father was unemployed for nearly ten years after arriving in New York. Living in the vicinity of poverty was one of the reasons Franci, herself, contemplated suicide.

When I was seven, my mother had a "nervous breakdown" and added a psychoanalyst to the list of doctors who treated the many ailments and conditions she had developed in the war. She sometimes collapsed at the end of a workday, and asked me to hold her while she sobbed. I did, knowing that this was a secret. Loving my mother included hiding parts of who she was, not remembering what I saw, not taking in what I heard. I felt proud to be chosen to take care of her. I was steeped in girls' books of tending the wounded — Little Women, Cherry Ames, Florence Nightingale. It was treachery to wish that my mother be like feisty Mrs. Korner or adventurous Marya Mannes.

Marya was a writer, a category second only to musician in my mother's hierarchy of human worth. During the war, she had traveled Europe as a spy. Now she was one of a handful of women journalists who expressed their opinions on TV. Marya ordered trousers and capes and didn't get upset when my mother consulted her notebook of measurements, and informed her that both her waist and hips were now two inches wider than when she first came to Frances Epstein, Inc. Marya never asked me if I had a boyfriend. Though she had been married three times, she seemed uninterested in the discussions of sex and romance that other customers pursued during fittings. She talked politics and books.

That earned her special status with my mother. Franci nursed a kind of contempt for the naïve girl she had been before the war and, now, for the customers who believed the version of love they saw in Hollywood movies. Her first husband, she often said, had been more of a playmate than a partner. They would have divorced had he not been murdered in the war. My father Kurt, on the other hand, was solid as a rock in a world that had been reduced to rubble.

She never talked about their first touch, their first dance, or first kiss — those significant moments that I read about in girls' lit. Theirs was, I later discovered, a fairly typical post-war marriage. There was no courtship; there was a housing shortage. One date at the swim club and 24 hours later they were living together. They met in June of 1946 and married that December. I was born eleven months later.

In February of 1948, there was a Communist coup. Kurt saw the Communists as Nazis in a different color uniform and was determined to get out. My prescient father had applied for an American visa right after returning to Prague from *koncentrák* and with the help of relatives in New York, we flew out of Prague and joined the Czech refugee community there.

Kurt was 16 years older than Franci and had briefly been one of her swimming coaches when she was a teenager. My mother said she had married him because he understood what she had been through and because the camps had broken neither his athletic discipline nor his old-fashioned good manners. It certainly was no disadvantage that he was tall, good-looking and well-connected. All that trumped the fact that he came from a small town while she was from Prague, that he was a life-long jock — an Olympic athlete — while she lived for the arts. My mother — who had considered jumping into an icy river on first New Year's Eve after liberation — married a swimmer.

Many such anomalous unions were called *"lager"* marriages because they were transacted in DP camps soon after the war and between survivors far less compatible than my parents. No matter how unlikely the partners, divorce was rare. The war served as marital glue and it was permanent. No refugee could afford divorce, my mother sometimes said. None viewed infidelity as reasonable cause. That was the kind of American nonsense her customers believed.

Robbie, it turned out, was largely unaware of all that. When he came to dinner, he thought I had an unusually happy family. Like many of my old friends, he was impressed that my father was an athlete and my mother ran her own business. In journalism school, my women friends whose mothers had been housewives envied my having had a mother who modeled how to have a marriage, three children, and a lifelong career.

I didn't argue with them. I understood that my mother's work structured her days, subsumed her illnesses, disappointments and unhappiness, and provided a creative outlet, but I didn't find her example particularly enviable. Between her *salon,* her kitchen and her family, she had no free time. She worked like a robot, often without pleasure, with no margin for error. She was not playful nor whimsical nor frivolous, and often exhausted. Her customers were difficult: many of them could not make up their minds what they wanted; many paid late or grudgingly or sometimes not at all. Some were unhappy and expected my mother to solve their problems with a blouse. Others were ill: they needed a therapist, not a dressmaker. They made her even more contemptuous than she already was of women.

On the rare occasions when my mother read me fairy tales, she would snap the book shut at the end as though to say that I should not count on being chosen or roused by a kiss or rescued. A girl had to be awake, not asleep, self-reliant not dependent, and not waiting passively for anyone to save her — let alone a prince. When American mothers gave their daughters elaborate Sweet Sixteen parties, mine gave me cash with which to travel abroad. Before I left, she handed me a prescription for birth control pills "in case." She didn't explain under what circumstances a "case" might present itself. She didn't discuss sexual feeling at all, but took me to the Italian film *Two Women,* in which a mother and daughter are raped by marauding soldiers during the second world war. Her message to me seemed clear. Being female meant being vulnerable. Matters of life or death could be determined in a split second. They had been.

In my married life as a mother of sons, I sometimes missed the conversation and the mix of smoke, powder and perfume in my mother's *salon.* But I had no desire to relive with a daughter the future I glimpsed during those afternoons of watching and talking with the customers. I had often wished I could stop time and not have to grow up to be a woman.

~ 6 ~

Robbie remembered the master bedroom, my mother's cutting table, her sewing machines and headless mannequins. Coming from a Communist family, it looked like a factory to him. He couldn't figure out where my parents slept. He wondered about their sexual life. "There was a lot of sexual energy coming off Franci," he said, but I didn't respond. I wasn't ready to discuss that yet.

Instead I asked whether he recalled how he'd become our weekly dinner guest.

"I must have insinuated myself into those Monday nights," he replied. "I was always on the lookout for a happy family. There was a sense of safety in your house that I didn't have in mine. You took it all for granted."

Insinuated himself? Surely Robbie had understood that my father's code of etiquette demanded that he reciprocate Robbie's driving me home after chorus. As far as safety, it had been Robbie who represented safety to me.

We lived on the tenth floor, a long elevator ride up and down. Because there was no doorman, anyone could walk into our building and did. I always strode purposefully from the street into the lobby to the elevator, checking the stairwell for intruders. If a strange man or boy was waiting to go up, I let him go alone.

Once, a delivery boy had followed me into the elevator. His hand was under my skirt, his mouth on mine as soon as the door closed. I pressed the alarm button, pushed him away and, when the elevator stopped, ran down the stairs.

I didn't tell my parents. They were both exhausted by dinnertime: my mother by her various ailments, customers, suppliers and seamstresses; my father by the grimy clothing factory where, after a decade of unemployment, he had finally landed a job. Given the extent of their problems, they didn't have much sympathy for mine.

But when Robbie came for dinner on Monday evenings, my father offered him cognac in our colored glasses from Czechoslovakia and, for a rare relaxed few hours, I felt we were normal, entertaining company, like people on TV. More typically, neighbors nodded to us in the elevator or exchanged a few sentences, but none ever rang our doorbell or came into our living room like Robbie or Vivian Vance on *I Love Lucy.*

My parents' friends were too formal to drop in and lived too far away. On birthdays, immigrant cousins from outside the city sometimes appeared, but they rarely spoke English and I could never figure out how we were related. Sometimes I felt like we lived in an outpost in outer space, the first batch of people to colonize the moon. For Robbie, I discovered, our apartment had been a kind of mecca.

"My first taste of Europe," he called it. He appreciated everything I took for granted: the formality, parental authority, the way we all sat down to eat at the same time, the hot, homemade food. "There was genuine interest in what children said — no condescension, no dismissal of their ideas. I liked being treated like a special person, someone worthwhile."

That was all true. We were expected to be seated at six sharp, when my mother put the meat and dumplings or potatoes and salad on the table. Robbie was unfailingly prompt, pleasant and engaging then, a 20th century Tom Sawyer. I imagined him tuning up his Chevy in his parents' driveway, near the white picket fence I thought surrounded all houses outside Manhattan. I imagined that his mother baked cookies and pies. He was always ready with a joke and a grin.

My parents didn't grin. You couldn't even count on them to smile like American parents did; they didn't recognize the cues. But Robbie didn't seem to notice. He talked to Franci about music, and to Kurt about sports and the news. They argued politics — Castro's Cuba, the Cold War, Vietnam, the civil rights movement. Robbie had never met a worker who disliked unions. He was shocked that Kurt, a card-carrying member of a progressive one like the International Ladies' Garment Workers' Union, viewed the union as racist and coercive. But Robbie basked in my father's attention. Kurt was responsible for the warmth in our house, he remembered.

Robbie even liked to look at my father's water polo albums. Nothing embarrassed me more than page after crumbling page of photos of hairy men in clingy bathing suits that clearly outlined their genitals, but Robbie listened as Kurt recited the scores of pre-war competitions in Budapest, Barcelona, and Algiers. He was particularly impressed by my father's stories of the Berlin Olympics where Kurt had played water polo and watched "the Negro athlete Jesse Owens," as my father called him, disprove Aryan racial theory by winning gold. He had even seen a woman break out of the stands and kiss a startled Hitler. "It would have been better if she had shot him," my father usually ended his story.

My mother was a whole other deal, Robbie recalled of those Monday evenings. "Sexy — not maternal. One wanted her approval which she never gave."

Yes, I thought, seeing facets of my family that I had grown so accustomed to that I no longer registered them.

My mother was one of those refugees who was also a snob, Robbie said, and I thought he was dead on. She grouped Americans into two categories: idiots and heroes. The heroes were the GIs who liberated the concentration camps, liberal journalists like Marya, musicians like Leonard Bernstein, and the doctors who helped manage the pain of her chronic illnesses. The idiots were the majority of Americans, uneducated people who believed that she had come to the U.S. looking to make money or that Prague was a backwater. Robbie reminded her of the GIs, grinning and tossing candy out at the populace as they drove their trucks through the ruins of Europe in 1945. When I told him, Robbie said he had, in fact, been named for his mother's first husband, a soldier who died in the invasion of Normandy and asked, "Do you think she viewed me as your suitor?"

Probably, I replied. He must have reminded Franci of her first love, an architecture student who had come to her parents' Prague apartment every week for dinner when she was a teenager. My mother was glad to have Robbie around, since I attended a high school for girls and, at 15, seemed to her skittish around boys.

When she was my age, Franci often noted, she and her cousin Kitty went to tea dances where they danced the tango and practiced flirting. I found flirting self-abasing as well as phony, and hated our high school dances where girls had to wait to be chosen by boys in order to dance. In 1963, dancing alone or with another girl was out of the question. If chosen, dancing meant sweaty hands on my back, unfamiliar smells, and pressure against my groin. The combination of being tall and obviously nervous kept boys away. After a few minutes of leaning against the gym wall surveying the dancers, I usually volunteered to carry trays of drinks and cookies.

So my mother was as delighted by my interest in Robbie as I was by his effect on my parents. Dinner at the Epsteins was usually scheduled with the precision of a train schedule and filled with unspoken tension. My mother and father asked the usual questions about school and then traded terse dispatches — news from the *salon* and garment district, finances, doctors' visits. My father was often in danger of being laid off. My mother's customers often owed her money; suppliers needed to be paid.

On Mondays, Robbie cheered everybody up. He downed the mug of beer my father offered him to wash down the dumplings and goulash. Robbie didn't seem rattled if the tattoo on my mother's forearm met his eyes as she served him or if she dropped the word *koncentrák.* I could ignore the early warning system I had developed to detect impending family storms. I could stop trying to anticipate disaster. I felt I had an ally, even a surrogate.

"I can't find the words to describe your mother's voice," Robbie said.

Of course not, I thought. Urgent, sardonic, with an edge of desperation. She didn't soften it for Robbie, but when he came to dinner, she wasn't likely to lock herself inside the bathroom, threaten suicide, repeat that she wanted to die.

When Robbie came over, I didn't have to cajole my mother into conversation, or write her notes and slip them under the door.

It was much, much later that I came to understand how surviving their war was understood to give my parents and their friends a blank check for behavior. Franci never acknowledged her suicidal episodes. Nor did my father acknowledge his sudden rages. PTSD was not a household word back then. Trauma was not a field of inter-disciplinary study. Franci held the franchise on pain in our family, physical and psychological. Her endless doctors' appointments, prescriptions, and pills attested to that. Other people's pain was ignored in our household. My father had been in the camps too but, for the most part, he kept the war contained. If something hurt me, I knew better than to complain. Disappointment didn't register as a problem. "Don't exaggerate!" both my parents said.

I sometimes wondered if they had never learned to formulate words for feelings in Europe, whether they lost the habit in the war, or whether they didn't feel comfortable expressing emotion in a language they had only come to use as adults. Their vocabulary didn't include words for sadness and pain, excitement or pleasure. Sometimes, my father would sing a line of an old Czech love song, but I don't remember either of my parents saying, "I love you." They avoided talk about feelings and cut me short when I expressed mine. Much later I came across the psychological term *alexithymia,* invented to describe people who had trouble identifying and naming feelings.

Robbie had no trouble expressing feelings. "Weren't you scared?" he might ask as my mother recounted one of her war stories.

My mother responded with her usual sarcasm. "What a question! If you had allowed yourself to be frightened, you were as good as dead."

Robbie seemed immune to the acidity of her tone.

"But I don't get it," he'd try again. "Weren't you terrified?"

I was shocked that he could challenge my mother. If I questioned her authority, I was ordered to my room. If she was at the end of her rope, she slapped me.

I thought all children were slapped. Kurt told us that we were more fortunate than he had been as a child: *his* father had used a leather strap, not a bare hand. I felt more insulted than physically hurt when I was slapped, but didn't reflect on those feelings then. I believed I didn't have the right to be angry at my parents. I certainly didn't hit back.

Parental violence seemed like a bad dream on those Monday nights. After dinner, I cleared the table. Then Robbie drove me to chorus and we sang for Mr. Labovitz. At break, Robbie would exchange stupid jokes with his pal. Then, he would drive me home.

"You were so quiet in the beginning," Robbie said. "I imagined all kinds of things."

I don't remember imagining much about Robbie. I accepted my parents' view that he was an American boy, a very gifted musician, perhaps a little too political for his own good. At first, I had no idea of where he was coming from when he arrived at our door for dinner and no inclination to ask. I knew that he practiced the piano, went to college, gave guitar lessons to children to earn money. It didn't occur to me to wonder whether he had a girlfriend. For a long time, I was content in the small space of our Mondays and untroubled by wanting more.

~ 7 ~

"Give Robbie my regards," my husband said, as formal as my father. Though not an athlete, Patrick is a tall, attractive European who in many ways resembles Kurt. Self-confident — some would say arrogant — self-disciplined, and reliable, he is also an uxorious man. He enjoys meeting my old boyfriends and wondering why I didn't marry them, claiming not to understand that they did not wish to marry me. By 2000, we had been holding hands through travels, births and deaths for almost two decades. Whenever I flew away, he drove me to the airport.

As I handed the attendant my boarding pass, I noticed her glance at my wedding ring that, along with my sensible haircut and shoes, suggested a steadfastness I did not entirely feel. On the plane, no one bothered to check if my seatbelt was fastened. I had finally become what I had so desperately wanted to be as a girl: invisible. From that safe place of invisibility, I was embarking on a quest.

Many people have a Robbie in their past but few of them decide to revisit him or her. My male friends were particularly wary of rekindling old flames. They didn't buy my explanation of searching out Robbie as an archive or muse. He was an old boyfriend. More than that: my first love. How could I put Patrick through this? they asked me.

My girlfriends offered theories about menopause and middle age, the waning of sexual drive, the lack of excitement in my life since our move to the suburbs. One even dreamt that I had gone to the races and put my money on a losing horse.

I wasn't sure why I had felt a need to delve into my adolescence with the help of Robbie, just that I needed to do it. If pressed, all I could come up with was a vague notion of wanting to revisit a time in my life I had only walked through — not truly experienced — and understanding why.

As my plane took off west across Massachusetts toward New York State, I took out my journal and a pen. But instead of writing, I pressed my face to the window and looked down at the landscape of the state in which I now lived. After two decades in New England, I was still, like Robbie in California, a New Yorker. My posture and stride, the way I talked and what I talked about were unmistakable.

Like Robbie, too, I had never imagined I'd ever live anywhere else but Manhattan. Everyone I knew — my parents, my teachers, my friends — believed that the smartest, most gifted and ambitious people in the world came to live in New York City. Why would anyone already there ever leave?

Unlike the unpredictable 21st century world of my sons' childhood, I grew up with a post-war illusion of stability that was broken only by President Kennedy's assassination. There was a nuclear arms race that threatened to destroy the world but an Iron Curtain clearly demarcated allies and enemies. In those days before the internet, we didn't hear much about local wars and massacres. Personal as well as national identities were clear-cut: a dress code clarified any person as old or young, male or female, rich or poor, Caucasian, Asian, Negro or what, in my neighborhood, we called Spanish. Even during a winter blizzard, my all-girls high school forbid wearing pants. Our teachers, like all women in America, wore skirts and dresses of identical length, their hemlines determined by authorities in Paris. Professional men dressed in suits and even factory workers like my father wore shirts and ties. Everyone slicked down unruly hair with pomade. Old or ripped clothing was a sign of poverty and considered unappealing.

Before identity politics made differences interesting and discussing them important, I was unaware that most of my classmates on the West Side were either the children of refugees from abroad or those in internal exile: American Communists. Family backgrounds were not considered topics of social or cultural interest. Very few of us talked about our families or their places of origin or their social class. We talked about what we wanted to become. Inspired by our President, I wanted to join the Peace Corps, then the Foreign Service, but from my base in New York. Everyone thought Robbie would become a famous musician like Leonard Bernstein.

President Kennedy's assassination was a massive shock to me and my friends. Some of them dropped out of school, rejected traditional trajectories, joined communes, ignored traditional sequences of establishing careers, marriages and families, and scattered like pick-up sticks across the country. Robbie dropped out of college to work in civil rights. I began leaving the country when I could.

When I mentioned that turning point to Robbie he said that, given the anti-Communist violence of his childhood, Kennedy's assassination had meant less to him than to me. He had been raised with FBI men knocking at his door, HUAC, strikes, and marches where people jeered at him and his parents. Despite or perhaps because my parents were so fixated on their war, he thought I had sleep-walked through the Sixties with little awareness of race and class.

That was true, I thought, hearing what he said without feeling it, the way I listened to my parents' stories. I had embraced only the parts of 1960s counter-culture that I chose. I resonated with the ideology of authenticity, and the natural look, dress and manners. I sang folk songs and went on the occasional march. But I was ignorant of the political background of the songs I sang, even the union songs. The crowds at marches made me uneasy. When Robbie went to Mississippi as a civil rights worker that summer of 1964, I left the country. France had been my first choice, but I had no money to live there. Mrs. Korner suggested a kibbutz in Israel; all I'd need was airfare.

For a 16-year-old girl to fly unaccompanied across the Atlantic had been unusual in 1964, I recalled as I flew west in 2000. Air travel was a luxury then: I remembered plush upholstered seats, real china, glass and silverware. My parents were delighted by my enterprise but unenthusiastic about my destination. They were Jews, but not Zionists. My father had had the misfortune of living in a small country surrounded by powerful neighbors and had paid for it twice — once because of Nazi Germany, once because of Stalin's Soviet Union. The United States was a country with oceans on two sides — one reason he had chosen it over Israel, he argued, was that Israel was another small country surrounded by powerful neighbors and perpetually at risk of extinction.

Kurt was unaware that at the Sunday School where he had sent my brother and me to learn about Judaism, one of my favorite things was gluing stamps of green leaves to the poster of a bare tree in our classroom, part of a campaign to reforest the new State of Israel. After he bought the novel *Exodus,* I read and re-read its 697 pages multiple times. I was eleven years old and impressed by its brave characters especially teen-aged Karen. She had survived the war and the British blockade to reach British-controlled Palestine, joined a kibbutz, and died for her ideals.

Israel was my age and as filled with adolescent idealism and illusion. At 16, I'd never seen such a blue sky or breathed air that smelled of citrus and the sea. There were so few cars in the country that you could stroll across the Tel Aviv-Haifa highway at noon. Most people traveled by bus or communal taxi or hitch-hiked. There were two radio stations, no TV. I saw that Arabs and Jews lived in separate towns and had little interaction but neither denied the existence of the other.

I lived in an old shack for kibbutz volunteers from abroad. I got up at 5 every day but Shabbat, and washed at an outdoor spigot. I worked in the peanut or sunflower fields weeding rows of plants. I liked the rural, egalitarian culture and, especially, the standard issue clothes. There was no fashion on kibbutz: everyone wore the same shorts, shirts and sandals. I didn't have to think about the way I looked or the way other people looked at me. Despite my father's warnings, I felt safer than I had ever felt in Manhattan. I learned some Hebrew and by the end of the summer, was wondering whether I might leave the country my parents had chosen and become an Israeli.

~ 8 ~

Robbie had spent the summer of 1964 in Mississippi, not far from where three other civil rights workers were murdered by the Ku Klux Klan. I don't remember Robbie mentioning anything about Mississippi when we resumed our Monday night dinners before chorus rehearsal. In my recollection, he preferred to question me about what I did on kibbutz and how socialism worked in Israel. None of his friends had traveled abroad alone and he was impressed that I had. He and my parents had long conversations about the presidential election that fall — President Lyndon B. Johnson was running against conservative Barry Goldwater and all three were worried.

Robbie urged me to write about what I was like when I came back from Israel. I had been all but oblivious, he said, to what was going on in the United States.

I took his cue and wrote.

I had been as idealistic a teenager as Robbie, but less ideological. Personal, everyday activism suited me better than collective action. And once I discovered what seemed to me egalitarian and unmaterialistic kibbutz life, I lost interest in America. In Israel, I had felt comfortable and if not entirely invisible, at least unremarked upon. Back in the U.S., I felt like a deer in the cross-hairs. It bothered me to live with daily whistles and catcalls, sexual comments from men in the street, or my parents' Czech friends, or my dentist. I understood them as threats.

That November of 1964, I was a tall, bodacious 17-year-old who felt and behaved like a little girl in the presence of men. Since age eleven, I had attended Hunter High School, the only public prep school for intellectually gifted girls in the country, and boys had largely disappeared from my daily life. But while many of my schoolmates bemoaned the absence of boys, I didn't. I found it restful. My best friend called me a "sexual retard." Although I had the adequate sexual equipment, she said, it didn't seem to be hooked up. I didn't understand what girls meant when they said they were "hot" or "horny," or had become so excited that they had "creamed their pants."

I recalled an episode in the Dinosaur Hall of New York's Museum of Natural History, intellectual home of celebrated anthropologist Margaret Mead, author of *Coming of Age in Samoa.* Whenever they could, our teachers tried to link our lives to those of brilliant women. Instead of hearing a lecture on Mead, a group of us peeled off to listen to our classmate Liane's experiences of coming of age in Manhattan. Her parents were divorced. No one was home in the afternoons. That was where she and her boyfriend made love.

I was accustomed to hearing Liane analyze poetry in English class. T.S. Eliot, Yeats, Dylan Thomas. She explicated the most obscure lines and images in a steady voice that was as mature and soft as her body. In the Dinosaur Hall, she talked about equally puzzling things: Erich Fromm's book *The Art of Loving* and the pleasures of sex with her boyfriend.

As the marble floor grew cold against my thighs — we were still obliged to wear skirts to school — part of me felt curiosity; another part, despair. Like my classmates, I had always had "crushes." I idolized friends, teachers, Robbie. But I had no experience of erotic feeling and was becoming aware of being left behind. Liane described a ladder of sexual intimacy with her boyfriend from kissing to French kissing to petting to intercourse but, to me, it was as though she was speaking Chinese.

No one sitting under that enormous dinosaur skeleton asked a single question. I assumed they all knew and had felt what she had.

My friends included many kinds of girls: jocks, science nerds, creative types, as well as girls who smoked, cut class, and trawled for men in Central Park. They considered me a leader and rebel — president of the debating club, writer of class plays and songs, sometimes an instigator of student protest. Few suspected that most things about sex scared me.

Though some of the girls in the Dinosaur Hall were already taking the new birth control pill, it was not discussed in school. Hunter's Sex Ed was behind the times, our lesbian students and faculty members still under the radar. In English class, we read *The Scarlet Letter* — not *Ulysses.* Girls' books and magazines were vague on practical sexuality. In that pre-internet time, a close-mouthed TV or movie kiss stood in for everything Liane was describing. The magazines I read at my doctor's office described women who liked sex as "nymphomaniacs" and women who didn't as "frigid." I wondered if Liane was in the first category and I was in the second.

I identified with Gigi, Colette's heroine, whose story was then a musical on Broadway. Gigi lived in Paris, with her courtesan mother and grandmother, but she managed to be oblivious to the sexual transactions taking place in her home. She warded off consciousness of her own sexuality and clung to a willful innocence.

My friends occasionally insisted I needed to get what we called "experience" and escorted me to a group called NEYO. The National Ethical Youth Organization was the youth group of a humanist institution that offered Friday night discussion groups and folk dancing to teenagers. Many dances were performed in lines or circles, eliminating the humiliation of waiting to be selected.

I quickly learned to put myself in the vicinity of Michael, a reasonably attractive boy who didn't dance or discuss great books. He was there to pick up girls and was so playful that I sometimes had an intimation of the fun to be had with boys.

I rarely had to wait long for Michael to suggest that we go to his car. Unlike Robbie, Michael never turned on the ignition. He just leaned over and began kissing my face and neck. I became unusually still. Numb. Then Michael slipped his hand inside my bra and moved his fingers around. He was slow and gentle but I felt unimplicated, as though he was kissing and stroking someone else. I also felt impatient, puzzled and worried.

"What did you do?" my friends asked afterwards, and, "Did you like it?"

I didn't know how to answer. Sometimes I zoned out and couldn't remember. Sometimes I could remember gestures but no sensations.

The most painful episode I remembered from my adolescence involved Robbie himself. He had organized a civil rights benefit in one of his hometown churches and asked me to sing in the chorus. After the concert, there would be a party and then he'd see to it that I got home all right.

I would have dived off the George Washington Bridge for Robbie; of course I would sing. I was also thrilled to be invited to the town in which he had grown up and to meet his friends. We sang the Fauré Requiem, a powerfully moving piece of music that I had not heard before. When it was over, we were all driven to a rich benefactor's home on the top of a hill overlooking the Hudson River.

I remember that suburban living room as clearly as I remember the Dinosaur Hall. I leaned against a piece of available wall, absorbing the scene as though I were a piece of photographic paper: the pastel-colored furniture; the rows of bookshelves; the paintings that were not reproductions. Robbie sitting in a wide pink easy chair that might as well have been a throne, joking with a bevy of girls who had draped themselves over the arms and back.

It dawned on me then that while Robbie knew almost everything about my life, I knew almost nothing about his. On those Mondays when he came for dinner, I glimpsed a mere sliver of his world. In that living room I realized that the perky soprano soloist was his girlfriend and that he was on intimate terms with several of the girls on the pink chair.

Anyone else, I thought, would have understood that Robbie had a string of girlfriends. Only I had been ignorant. Those other girls felt comfortable claiming his attention, even a space on that pink chair. I, on the other hand, felt paralyzed. It was devastating to discover that my experience of Robbie was partial and humiliating to learn that while I adored him, he clearly adored someone else.

I don't know how I got home. I didn't tell anyone about the evening. I felt invisible but, perhaps for the first time as a teenager, unhappy about it.

~ 9 ~

Those clips from adolescence played in my mind as I flew west to meet Robbie. All now seemed precursors of the uncanny experience I had shared with him a few years later when I turned 20. It had been so eerie and troubling that, three decades later, I was still puzzling over it. Maybe it was the main reason I had reconnected with Robbie.

All of 1968 was filled with violence, assassinations, arrests and many kinds of political disturbances — in the U.S. and Europe, everywhere but Israel, where I was at university studying musicology and English literature and planning a summer trip to Prague.

Western tourists did not often tour countries behind the Iron Curtain back then. Americans needed visas and visas were often denied. Czechoslovakia was in the throes of a widely watched political liberalization in the spring of 1968; it was thought that the Soviet Union would not tolerate its experiment of "socialism with a human face." But I paid little attention. On August 16, I took the train from Vienna to Prague.

I looked out my window at the barbed-wired No-Man's-Land between Austria and Czechoslovakia for what seemed an eternity. The Czech border guards were hostile. Coldly, they studied passports, searched bags, and removed passengers from compartments. I worried because my passport noted Prague as my birthplace, and was relieved when the train began moving again.

As we pulled into Prague's Central Station, I heard Czech blare from loudspeakers and spew from the mouths of black marketeers looking for dollars and jeans. Nothing had prepared me for hearing my family language from strangers.

My hosts looked and sounded like my parents, treated me as though I were an heirloom, and squabbled over where I would stay. I no longer felt tall. I looked like most other young women on Prague streets, long-legged, slim-hipped, full-breasted. As I wandered about the city in a happy daze, the spires and colors seemed deeply familiar. Did I remember gazing at those gray and ochre walls as I lay on my back in my pram? I was slated to move from one doting family to another on August 21 when, before it was light, my hosts woke me with the words, "We're occupied."

"That's OK," I said sleepily, thinking they meant, "We're busy." Then I heard shots and understood that they meant "occupied by an army."

They told me that I couldn't call my parents because international phone lines had been cut. They needed to stock up on food and gas and left, ordering me to stay inside. I got dressed and went out.

I stood on the corner of their street and a large avenue, watching a line of Soviet tanks roll toward me. My eyes registered the soldiers standing on top of the tanks, behind machine guns; my ears heard the sickening crunch of cobblestones. But I felt nothing until my knees buckled beneath my body and I almost fell. I translated that knee buckling into the word "scared," and went back inside. I listened to the radio, saw a typewriter, and sat down to type what I had seen and heard.

I made a copy of what I had typed, then folded each text into an envelope. I addressed the envelopes "To the Editor of the *Jerusalem Post*" and "To the Editor of the *New York Times*". I had no street address for either. To Jerusalem and New York.

Local phones were still working and my mother's cousin Kitty phoned to tell me that the American Embassy had organized an evacuation of U.S. citizens by special train to Paris. She spoke in slow, simple English. I should pack my luggage and walk across the river to her part of the city. I should be very careful crossing the bridge. There were soldiers. She would be waiting on the other side. It was important to start walking right away.

I lugged my suitcase past tanks, people waving flags, walls defaced with anti-Soviet graffiti. My suitcase had no wheels; I had to stop every few minutes to rest. When I finally got to the river, I saw soldiers standing on their tanks, two tanks on each side of the bridge, manning machine guns. I walked across the bridge like a duck in a penny arcade, thinking anyone could shoot me without consequence, still feeling nothing but registering every detail.

Kitty, who had survived *koncentrák* with my mother, was waiting for me. I gave her everything in my suitcase, including my favorite polka-dot dress. The next day, she took me to the train station from which she and my mother and father and most of Prague's Jews had been deported to the camps. She had obtained a window seat for me on the evacuation train, gave me a bag of sandwiches and a large bottle of water. Then she kissed me good-bye and said I should kiss my mother for her.

When I arrived in Paris 26 hours later, I accosted strangers and asked them for stamps. I pasted as many as I could fit onto the two envelopes I had prepared and mailed my personal account of the Soviet Invasion of Czechoslovakia to the two newspapers. Strangers took me in, and as I marked time before my charter flight home, I watched television footage of the invasion interspersed with footage of the violence in Chicago at the Democratic National Convention. Two weeks later, I was waiting to board the plane home to New York, when I overheard two passengers discussing an article one had read in the *Jerusalem Post* about the invasion — by an American girl trapped in Prague.

~ 10 ~

I don't remember reuniting with my parents, just with Robbie. He's parked by a fire hydrant on 79th Street facing west toward Riverside Drive and the Hudson River. I tell Robbie what I'm unable to tell my parents: how scared I was in the Soviet invasion; how I had felt walking across that bridge and being evacuated from a war zone when the people who had taken care of me couldn't leave; how lonely I felt in Paris.

Then, I ask if he'll sleep with me.

What? He says, in 1968.

What? I think in 2000. Did this actually happen? Did it happen this way?

At first, Robbie is cautious. What's this about? He wants to know. True, he has no girlfriend at the moment. But what will happen afterwards? I'm going back to college in a few weeks, am I not?

I'm flying back to Israel in two weeks. So what? I'm twenty years old, not a virgin. What's there to think about? For years he's been sleeping with other girls; why *not* me?

We argue in the car while the sun sets.

Well? I say when it's gone.

Robbie turns the key in the ignition and drives to his mother's house in the Bronx.

I lost my virginity at Hebrew University, chose one of the young Israelis who cruised the foreign girls' dorms to "improve their English."

His name was Uri. We had several conversations before, one night, he leaned over to kiss me. I confessed that I had never had sex before.

At all? Uri exclaimed. Rising to the occasion, Uri had directed me to take a shower and return in a nightgown. Then he told me to lie down beside him on my narrow bed and let him know if anything hurt. Nothing hurt, but I didn't feel much of anything. The earth didn't move. The action seemed enigmatic and far away, as though through the wrong end of a telescope.

When he was done, he instructed me to take another shower. I did that; he got dressed, kissed me and left. I felt as though I had graduated girlhood in the dark.

It's dark when we arrive at Robbie's mother's house. Robbie takes my hand and leads me to the basement door, switches on a light. I see a washing machine, a shelf of colored candles burning, a large rumpled bed.

How did we get from the door to the bed? I have no idea. Does Robbie kiss me? Undress me? I have no recollection. We must have moved, we weren't statues, but I don't remember moving. Robbie must have felt like he was making love to one of my mother's mannequins because I hear his voice, not soft nor wry but angry.

What's going on? First I talk him into this. Now I'm not there.

I get angry back. He's supposed to know what he's doing. He's got years of experience — not me.

"Get on top of me," he says quietly.

I've never sat naked on a man with his penis inside me before. For a moment I'm flooded with sensation that later I will learn to expect and enjoy. I feel high up in the air, like on the back of a camel lurching over the desert, sand dunes shifting under me. It's very hot. I'm going to melt away like the candles. But then, something even scarier happens.

The part of my body above my waist detaches like the first stage of those multi-stage rockets that carry astronauts into space. Then my consciousness or soul, whatever part of me it is that negotiates the world, shoots out of my skull and is floating in the blackness near the ceiling. My eyes are up there too. I'm looking down at my body as though from a satellite. I see the top of my head, my hair spread out over my shoulders and down my back, my body sitting astride Robbie's body, and nothing, no net, no parachute in that black void between where I am and where my body has remained. It's terrifying. How will I get back into my body?

Suddenly I'm no longer up there but on the sheets alongside Robbie, sobbing.

Robbie strokes my hair and says, "Shhh... It's all right... It's all right."

"It's not all right. I wasn't there," I'm finally able to stammer. "Nobody was there."

"Maybe you had an orgasm," he says. "I think you stopped breathing." Instead of looking worried, Robbie looked pleased. When I got back home, I wrote the word "orgasm" in my diary in Hebrew to keep it secret from my mother.

I never left my body again when we made love that fall. Neither did I feel much sensation. My pleasure came from being with Robbie. I was intensely happy a month later, didn't think twice about getting on the plane back to Israel. Only after I landed did I feel as though my skin would peel off if I touched another man. I focused on going to my classes in musicology and English literature. I began working for the newspaper that had published my account of the Soviet Invasion.

During my last year in Jerusalem, Arab terrorists planted explosives in the cafeteria where I ate lunch and the supermarket where I shopped. An iron fence was built around campus; inspections of handbags and backpacks — the kind that would become routine in most 21st century cities — began in Israel. I started paying more attention to my father's geopolitical concerns.

"I decided to move to the United States so that you could grow up in freedom," Kurt wrote. "We were a little tired after the war and, were it not for you, we probably would not have emigrated.

As a 'survivor' I am above all interested in avoiding any further sacrifice of our family. I want my children to live in peace."

I was accepted to journalism school and flew back to New York — and to Robbie, I thought. What could break a connection I felt sure was cosmic?

Manhattan shocked me after the stillness of Jerusalem: noisier, dirtier, and more dangerous than I remembered. But seeing Robbie had been even more shocking. He was unkempt in the lefty male style that had come into fashion while I was abroad. His mother had died; he had dropped out of music school and was composing for his rock band. He no longer took piano lessons or sang with Mr. Labovitz, but gigged at dives and weddings. He had another girlfriend now — or maybe two or three. I understood that he felt no cosmic connection between us. I was a friend, a good friend, but in the end just another girl who had been in his life and left. On occasion, we slept together in the casual way of the Sixties. I never raised the subject of the first time.

That had been 30 years before, I kept reminding myself as my plane began its descent. We were both now past 50. Whatever used to light up between us couldn't consume me anymore. Maybe Robbie wouldn't even recognize me. Over the phone I'd blurted out: "I've cut my hair; it's short."

Robbie had laughed. "I know you."

Did he?

As I wheeled my suitcase into the terminal, I scanned the people waiting. Then I spotted him — was that really Robbie?

His hair was gray, his body wide. He looked like a fat old woman.

I let him take my suitcase, slowed my stride to match his shuffle, chattered to hide my dismay.

Then I was sitting in his car and feeling the old delight. Like a duckling imprinted to its mother, I was still attached to Robbie in some fundamental and irreversible way.

"Do I look the same to you?" I asked.

“Yeah,” he said, pulling out onto the road. “Except you’re not naïve anymore.”

I hope not, I thought. I sure hope not.

~ 11 ~

I assumed that Robbie would book me a cozy B & B but he turned off the highway at a large neon arrow that read “Motel.”

Two floors of rooms built around a parking lot, an empty swimming pool, a shabby office with coffee and doughnuts left standing since breakfast. As I watched the manager appraise the two of us I thought I’d never choose a place like this to house myself or anyone I know.

Motels evoke an incongruous mix of associations: happy family travel, illicit sex, and cinematic murder. The prospect of staying in this motel scared me, but I didn’t want to offend Robbie nor feel afraid. So I took my key and suitcase up the concrete stairway. The door lock worked, and the room, with its popcorn ceiling and flowery turquoise décor, looked clean.

I locked the door behind me, went back downstairs and got back into the car.

“I need protein,” Robbie declared, and drove to a McDonald’s. He ordered a cheeseburger and fries, then asked if I wanted anything. When I shook my head, he said, “Don’t sigh, Helen. It’s bad karma.”

Robbie had introduced me to street food and to the amusements of Coney Island. He bought me a turn at the penny arcade where sinister-looking men hawked rifles and beckoned customers to shoot at revolving rows of wooden ducks. He talked me into riding the Cyclone and sitting on the very front bench, then laughed at my terror as the car climbed up the rails and plunged down like death. When we finally leveled out and slowed to a halt, I threw up into the nearest trashcan. He bought me a stick of pink cotton candy.

"You're such a snob," Robbie said as we sat at the McDonald's drive-in window. "Salads. Fish! Just because something swims in the ocean doesn't mean it's good for you. Don't you think about the garbage people dump in?"

I opened my notebook and took out my pen.

"I guess we're not losing any time."

"We don't have much."

The drive-in clerk passed his order through the car window. He unwrapped his cheeseburger, pulled onto the road, and asked, "What's the question?"

I had so many: I wanted him to tell me what I had been like as a girl, explain why he had become so involved with me and my family, and most important — if he remembered the night we had sex and I left my body. But I couldn't start there. So I began with questions about him. He was my prime witness. I needed to know where he came from.

"So where and when were you born?"

"Hollywood. Summer of 1945," he replied.

I actually hadn't known that. But Hollywood was, then as now, filled with people who came from and left for elsewhere.

His mother's people, Robbie said, were ranchers who owned their town by the time she was born. Blonde, blue-eyed, Tess studied theater in college, "fell in with the Stanislavski crowd," and, Robbie said, "got involved with a series of left-wing men."

She met his father Maury Ross in wartime Hollywood. Maury was from the Bronx, a writer and committee-Communist, who didn't go to college, "talked about the Spanish Civil War but didn't go, and managed to stay out of the Second World War, too."

No wonder Robbie had been so interested by my father, I thought. Robbie had been named for Tess's first husband, an actor and GI who had been killed on the beach during the American invasion of Normandy. Tess had been a widow when she met Maury, who had left a wife and daughter back in New York. "Everyone fell in love with my father," Robbie said. "Men as much as women... sometimes more. He was passionate, disarming, intense, charismatic."

Robbie crumpled the remains of his food into the bag between our seats and changed the subject. He didn't want me to use his parents' real names in a book. Naming names was a loaded issue in his family. Besides, he said, with more than a touch of resentment, "I've told you all this stuff. You never wanted to hear it."

I remembered Robbie's disdain for what he called my "magic house" and my lack of interest in Americans, but felt sure that he had never told me anything about his parents. But maybe I had forgotten what I wasn't supposed to know or didn't want to know? Mrs. Labovitz sometimes alluded to Robbie's "troubled" family as I helped her clean up after recitals, but I hadn't asked any questions. It wasn't done then and, besides, every refugee family I knew was "troubled."

I assured Robbie that I would use pseudonyms for him and everyone in his family.

When the House Committee on Un-American Activities began investigating Communists in Hollywood, he continued, Maury decided to look for work in television, in New York, telling Tess that he'd send for her and the kids when he was settled. By the time she arrived with Robbie and his younger brother, Maury was living with a young actress. He told Tess that she could accept it or sue for divorce. She chose divorce.

During the early 1950s, Robbie and his brother were shuttled between Maury's penthouse on Central Park West, in a building so full of important Communists that it was called "the Kremlin," and his mother's tenement in Hell's Kitchen. It was situated, he said, above a mattress factory "with a toilet in the hall" and occasional visits from the FBI.

By 2000, I knew enough about the history of American Communism to contextualize these details, but I felt sure he had never told me them before and I was surprised. We had lived one neighborhood away from Hell's Kitchen then. My father was largely unemployed, but we always had our own bathroom. And no FBI men ever questioned my parents or asked our neighbors to inform on them.

Robbie reminded me that there had been hundreds of families like his on the West Side. They had lived in my building. They had been in my classes at school. Had I never heard of the Rosenberg trial?

I reminded him that I was three when Julius and Ethel Rosenberg were indicted for espionage; five, when they were electrocuted. As a child in a Czech-speaking household, I didn't even understand that there were Communists living in the United States, any more than there were Nazis. I didn't remember anyone talking about McCarthy except, possibly, my mother's customers. When one of my favorite classmates disappeared from school in the 1950s, no one explained that his father had to move the family to England so he could work.

"The Reds I knew were decent people," Robbie said quietly. "They were the opposite of Nazis. My father's friends were men like your father. They worked hard. You would have liked Maury. Everyone did."

Unlikely, I thought and asked if we could take a walk.

"I can't walk," he said. "Try to remember that."

Why did I keep forgetting? Robbie had told me several times before I flew out west that he had chronic fatigue syndrome. I didn't want to believe it and didn't remember.

"How about coffee?" I asked, and he drove to a café.

Before the end of the 1950s, Tess and her third husband moved out of Manhattan to a town where he was a union organizer at the automobile plant. Tess gave birth to a baby girl and, "it was clear she was retarded."

Robbie and his brother commuted between homes and social class: weekdays in the working-class Tarrytown flats; weekends in the penthouse overlooking Central Park. The Kremlin Communists were mostly writers and actors. Some, like Maury, were blacklisted and wrote TV scripts using a "front."

Self-protective secrecy, I thought, might explain Robbie's reticence about his family when he came over for dinner on Monday evenings. The blacklist wasn't yet history. Many blacklisted Communists had left the U.S. or died or killed themselves. Others changed their names and occupations. Robbie would have been uneasy sharing his background with my anti-Communist parents. Nearly forty years later, I felt sure he was telling me about it for the first time.

Maury's third wife was the only parent who noticed that Robbie was drawn to the piano. "In the left-wing community, the piano was bourgeois, not a people's instrument like the harmonica or guitar or banjo," he said. But his step-mother Rose persuaded Maury to buy two pianos — one for their home, one for Tess's apartment. Rose was the one who, through the West Side left-wing network, found Mr. Labovitz.

"I loved her," Robbie said, and I was moved by the tenderness in his tone. He had almost routinely said, "I love you Helenka" when we said good-bye. I, on the other hand, rarely said, "I love" out loud, even to my husband and sons. It reeked of danger to me.

"When she split for Hollywood, Rose wrote us out of her resume," Robbie continued. "It didn't matter that I stood by her when she and my father fought, or that I used to carry messages between them when they weren't speaking. She left and it was like we never existed."

At the time Robbie was coming to eat dinner with my family, I calculated, Tess, his step-father, brother, and disabled half-sister had moved to the Bronx. Rose and his half-sister were living in Hollywood; Maury lived alone in the Kremlin; his first wife and Robbie's older half-sister lived somewhere else. That was what Mrs. Labovitz had meant by a troubled family.

The Kremlin Communists frequented a left-wing summer colony where, at the age of 14, Robbie was appointed Music Counselor, teaching and conducting children. He had picked up conducting from Mr. Labovitz. It hadn't been hard, he said, to take care of children after taking care of adults. In that way, he said, he was like me.

Suddenly, I remembered Maury's apartment. The terrace overlooking Central Park. A black leather couch and white rug. A framed photograph of Maury on the baby grand. "It looked like a lay-out from *Playboy,"* I said. "All that was missing was a Bunny."

"There was a Bunny for a while," Robbie said, grimly.

"Did you invite me there to impress me or sleep with me?"

"You? You were fifteen, but a fifteen that was five inside. The chemistry was there, but you seemed completely unaware of it. Part of your attraction was that you didn't know you were sexy."

Sexy. A word from my mother's *salon* that always made me uneasy. I felt I had heard enough information for one day. I needed time to process it. It was evening by the time he dropped me off at my motel. I went up the crumbling concrete steps, relieved that Patrick couldn't see where I was staying as I called home to tell him good-night. I checked that my motel room door and windows were locked, washed up, and went to bed.

~ 12 ~

Over the next three days, Robbie drove down back roads and we retraced our trajectories since the 1960s. After Mississippi, Robbie never returned to the track that led to Carnegie Hall while I used my musicology and journalism degrees to carve out a reporting niche at the Sunday *New York Times.* I wrote profiles of classical musicians — the brilliant, charismatic, celebrated men everyone thought Robbie would become. I spent hours in restaurants, rehearsal rooms, and small planes, conducting interviews during which, in the guise of journalism, I asked any question I chose. My interviewees were gifted performers who did their best to seduce their audience of one. Sometimes we became infatuated with one another and sometimes we didn't but I always felt intensely alive. Those interviews were like dreams of conversations I imagined having with Robbie.

I couldn't live on freelancing, so I found a job teaching journalism. Token woman; tenure track; a career path laid out like a map; everything Robbie refused.

He continued to earn a living by teaching music, playing gigs, composing, and producing the recordings of other musicians. In the 1970s, he had written an important music textbook; in the 1980s, became a respected music reviewer. But I was — unreasonably but deeply — disappointed that Robbie had not, as I saw it, done what he was born to do. And since he rarely told me anything about causative circumstances, I didn't understand why not.

Robbie had, I realized in retrospect, made reference to his emotional state on occasion, but each time he did, I had listened while refusing to take it in.

"My whole family's had to battle my manic thing," he said now as we drove. "It makes them crazy that I don't observe boundaries; they're afraid they'll go off the deep end. But what's manic anyhow if 60% of creative people are manic depressives? If I write a book in four weeks, is that a manic episode? If I hear an entire song complete with tune and all the lyrics, is that a manic episode? I think I've had manic episodes with you."

I tried hard this time to register what he said.

"I'm stabler now but stupid. I take my meds. I don't have mood swings. I am better. The immune system doesn't like ups and downs. It takes away mystical experience but the bottom line is that I'm 55 years old and I want to be nice to my wife and dog."

I laughed as he intended me to but vowed to remember that he had told me he was manic. When we were teenagers, it had been his younger siblings — certainly not Robbie — who were mentally fragile. After both his parents died when he was still in his 20s, Robbie felt responsible for them. But he hadn't told me much about any of his feelings at the time. He had many other confidants: always one serious relationship going, several back-ups, and a waiting list. One Valentine's Day in the 1980s, he showed up at my door wearing a wedding band. I had never heard of the woman he married.

I was 32 then, with relatively few short-term boyfriends and two live-ins behind me. The second one, a fellow journalist, had just moved out. Robbie glanced at the empty spaces in my bookshelves and, possibly to cheer me up, said he wanted to see the cottage I had bought with my first book advance.

Unlike my ex, who worried about money and success, and was uncomfortable enjoying the fruits of mine, Robbie had no trouble driving my car to my new cottage. He seemed thrilled with the way I had put a life together. "Just look at it," he said. "You're a college professor! You've published a book! You're a success!"

Right, I thought. Spending Valentine's Day with my long unrequited — now married — first love.

"You didn't want to marry Literary Man did you?" Robbie asked as he drove, and laughed when I confessed I had.

"Why?" he demanded.

Because, at 32, I felt a failure at intimacy. Though I had straightened out my erotic issues with my first ex — a graduate of Dr. Helen Singer Kaplan's course in sex therapy — and enjoyed what I thought was a full sexual life, I wanted it to be validated by marriage. The only person who had ever shown serious interest in marrying me was my rich old bachelor cousin whom Mrs. Lewis had urged me to consider when I was a teenager.

Robbie said it might surprise me to know he had been jealous of every boy I ever talked about.

"There weren't many," I replied. "And you always had a girlfriend."

"So what? I wanted you all to myself."

I had stared out the windshield. How had I missed this? This was news so stunning that, for a moment, it lit up my gloom.

"Why didn't you let me know?"

"I couldn't sleep with you casually," Robbie said, "That would have ended our friendship. And I wasn't going to sleep with you exclusively. Besides, I didn't know you were in love with me. You never came on to me. And even when you finally did, you said 'Look, it's not going to be the first time. Some Israeli soldier stood me up in a doorway and fucked me for three minutes so it's not like I'm a virgin or anything.'"

I blushed. I could feel the blood vessels dilating all over my skin.

"I didn't say 'fuck,'" I finally said. "He wasn't a soldier and I wasn't standing up."

"Sorry. But whatever you said, it wasn't poetic."

Poetic. No, my first time hadn't been poetic.

"Why did you get married?" I changed the subject.

"She's European. She wanted it. Her parents wanted it." Then, he gave me one of his sidelong looks and said, "I never got the feeling that your parents wanted you to get married or even that you did. But if you want to, it doesn't matter to whom. Find some European who'll support your writing. You don't need to discuss philosophy with him."

Robbie disappeared after that Valentine's Day. The next time I saw him, he was divorced and I had met Patrick.

In 2000, we parked in an empty lot, the Pacific Ocean spread out before us. Robbie sank down on a bench and said I didn't have to keep him company. "Go take a run."

I ran along the ocean, recalling my father's belief that sea air was natural medicine. He had also said, observing me with Robbie, that if I married him, I would have unhealthy children.

Like Robbie, Kurt had a "slow" younger sibling. I had never given much thought to my father's history and relationships — I was more focused on my mother's. Now I wondered what he had known about Robbie's family. Long before health became an American obsession, Kurt had maintained his body the way other men maintained their cars: with a regimen of country air, good diet, exercise, sleep and sex. Unlike other men, he talked about sex without innuendo, drama or sentiment. If a person had acne, thinning hair, or a paunch, my father thought more sex was the remedy.

Occasionally I got the sense that my father wanted more sex with my mother than she wanted with him. But he didn't seem to feel it as a pressing issue. My parents were by far the most attractive couple at the refugee gatherings in our living room, everyone smoking and eating Viennese pastries. My mother glittered in a dress of her own design, her gestures wreathed in smoke, performing an erotic ballet. A man would extend a packet of cigarettes, two or three protruding from the top. She would select one and put it to her lips, then lean forward for a light. The man — my godfather Ivan maybe, I thought on that California beach — snapped open his lighter. Sometimes he cupped a hand around the flame; sometimes she cupped his hands between her own. Both inclined their heads as though they were going to kiss, then my mother inhaled deeply and blew out a stream of smoke.

Even 50 years after the fact, in 2000, this memory made me queasy. I ran back toward Robbie. He hadn't budged from his bench.

He said he'd been thinking about why he had told me so little about himself back then. "After Mississippi," he said, "I was a different person. Then my father died and it felt like the world ended. Then my mother got sick and died. No one knew she was going insane. It wasn't manic depression — that was my father's side of the family."

He was saying so much so fast that the words "manic depression" slipped by me again. "And let's not forget the draft," Robbie swerved to the war that had affected, in one way or another, every young man I knew. He had stayed up for three nights running and thought of ways to act crazy, but in the end, classical music had saved him. The physician who examined him had an accent like my mother's. He saw that Robbie was a musician and asked whether he liked the composer Bruckner.

Robbie told him he loved Bruckner and got a deferment, "while all those other guys got drafted."

As far as his own composing was concerned, he had spent many months writing a cello sonata. A friend performed it twice, then no one played it again. "The End," he said. Then he was asked to compose his first commercial job — 20 seconds of music for NASA. He earned $3,000 in less than two hours. "That made it hard to stay with classical music."

Deaths of his parents, responsibility for his sibs, the war, and the need to earn a living. Enough to derail anyone, I thought as we walked back to his car.

"Marrying Kate was the best thing I ever did in my life. Maybe late, but the best thing," he said. "For years, I moved through girlfriends and didn't stay with anyone. I tended to punish women I liked — it was very destructive and it took me a long time to own up to."

Was he apologizing to me? I wondered.

Kate was making dinner when we drove into Robbie's driveway. I had met her years before, when she was Robbie's student, a teenager with braces on her teeth. I had felt such jealousy; now, only curiosity. She had become a performer and professor. Like me, she had married late after a relationship with Robbie that had been on and off for decades.

What did she think about my spending the day with her husband while she was working? And what did I think? Kate was gracious, cordial but careful. She was a performer, after all, and she was performing the role of impeccable hostess. I tried to be an admiring guest and, in fact, I admired her for having been able to create a life with Robbie.

Back in my motel room that evening, I turned on the TV and caught an old movie whose swelling soundtrack was familiar though I couldn't name it. Set in the Manhattan of my childhood, it was filled with familiar clothes, cars, and streets and it made me weep. The title was *An Affair to Remember* and I thought I was weeping because I was finally putting my long involvement with Robbie to rest. It didn't occur to me that the title of the movie referred as much to a love affair of my mother's as it did to mine with Robbie.

~ 13 ~

Students filled only about a third of the college auditorium where I gave a talk about writing family history and addressing trauma. Robbie chose a seat smack in the middle of a vacant zone, looking up at the stage. As I spoke, I noted our reversal of roles: his watching me closely at the podium the way I used to watch him when he conducted.

I talked about the writer's role of bearing witness to histories that had not been made public, and the ways I pursued archival and library research, identifying live sources and interviewing them. Having Robbie in my audience gave new meaning to my old talk. I forgot about the rest of my audience. I spoke directly to him.

"You're way too good for this place," he said as we left. "They should have done some publicity!" After I thanked him for his indignation, he volunteered that he was trying to write a family history of his own. He wanted to show me some documents and discuss how to piece together contradictory and complicated versions of a narrative.

At his house, he pulled out a carton, found a worn scrapbook and told me it was his mother's. I felt moved to hold it in my hands and more than a little intrusive paging through Tess' hand-pasted letters and newspaper clippings, photographs and poems. As I read her small-town newspaper story about Robbie's civil rights organizing, I could sense him monitoring my reactions. "When my mother unraveled, she told me a lot of stuff. I didn't really understand that she was going insane but when you go through her letters you see it."

Both of us had grown up with mothers who broke down, I thought. Both of us had become their caretakers.

"At first, she wouldn't sign for me to go to Mississippi," he said.

Of course not, I thought. He handed me a copy of a typed, single-spaced court transcript. I tried to comprehend the legalese but could not and looked up at Robbie scrutinizing my face. "They charged me with pointing a gun at an officer of the law," he said when I said I couldn't understand it. "They called me Jew-boy, nigger-lover. They knew exactly who I was, who my father was, the address on Central Park West. 'You a musician?' the guards would say. 'You like your hands?' They put you in the white jail and let it be known that at the end of 90 days they want you alive, but unable to use your hands..."

I held the transcript in my hands and didn't know what to say. "I'm sorry," seemed lame and inadequate.

"Just read it," he said, and I tried but got lost and started again. It happened a second time and a third. I could understand each word but couldn't process the meaning of the sentences. "I'm so close to these documents," he said. "I had to plead guilty to something I didn't do..."

That was the last thing I wrote down in my notebook. I don't remember how I responded or when I replaced all the papers into the carton and asked that he take me back to the motel.

On the last day of my visit, Robbie and Kate drove me to a waterfall that they liked to show to visitors. Kate sat in the front seat; I moved to the back. Robbie later told me that I began to chatter non-stop — so fast and in such an unfocused way that both he and Kate wondered what was going on.

I chattered all the way up to the waterfall. A dirt path led from the parking lot to a ravine where a log barrier prevented visitors from getting any closer to the water streaming down gray boulders into a bowl of rocks.

Three people were standing by the barrier. As we approached, a man and woman climbed over it and down into the gorge. They stood almost beneath the cascade of water posing for a man with a camera.

I felt sure the two would lose their footing, slip into the stream and drown. I saw their bodies floating away. "They're going to die!" I heard myself call out. I thought I had screamed but, Robbie told me later, I had whimpered.

He put his arm around me and asked, "What's up?"

I didn't know, but I found it hard to breathe.

"Those people are going to die," I managed to say again.

"Maybe you're having a panic attack," Robbie said.

I tried to say I'd never had a panic attack but I couldn't find the words. I wasn't sure I was speaking out loud, or even in English. I seemed to have lost every sense but sight.

Robbie scrutinized my face. "Those people are just posing for a photograph. Look, they're climbing back up."

"Someone's going to die here," I heard myself insisting. "Or someone did."

Robbie led me to a bench. "No one died here," he said in his most soothing voice. "You must be remembering something."

I remembered being very young, standing at the end of a rock jetty as the Atlantic Ocean roared in. I was three or four, holding onto the hand of my Czech nanny, watching the tide crash against the gray boulders, throwing up foam and streaming over the seaweed-covered rocks. I slipped, lost her hand, fell into a slimy crevice of the jetty.

Had I actually fallen? Into the ocean or just into the rocks?

I tried to tell this to Robbie but I couldn't find the words. He just wanted to calm me down. He said that the waterfall was one of his favorite places. No one had ever, as far as he knew, fallen into the stream. Many people posed for photographs. It was a favorite destination of lovers. I listened to the sound of his voice and tried to calm down.

"Are you okay now?" he asked after a while.

I said I was. The next day I flew back east to what I regarded as real life.

~ 14 ~

It was a relief to slide back into the clear-cut roles of wife and mother. There was nothing left in the fridge, Patrick said. We had to stop at the supermarket. I was pleased to return to competence: remember what was in the freezer, throw together a meal. Our dog welcomed me back, as did my sons. After dinner, they cleared the table without prodding. Absence had made everyone feel fonder. Patrick and I went to bed, made love, and then we caught each other up on the week.

I didn't tell him about the motel or the waterfall. Despite his optimistic outlook on the world, Patrick worried about my every cough. I rationed the number of potentially anxiety-provoking things I told him. I wanted to be the opposite of my mother, to protect my family from the messy, scary commotion in my emotional life. I fell asleep curled against my husband's body, thinking that in the morning I would wake up and everything would be back in place.

But something big had fallen out of place out west. If I had imagined that seeing Robbie would finally close a door left ajar, I had been wrong: instead, my visit had blown it open.

I had, by then, read reports of people who reconnected with their first loves and thought, at first, that what had happened to me at the waterfall was a consequence. Sociologists and psychologists reported disruption, even divorce as a consequence of such reconnections. All described the wild surge of adolescent emotions that could overpower the people involved.

I felt pleased to be reclaiming age-appropriate reactions that I had not entirely registered and understood when I was a partially numbed-out teenager. I felt "normal" and finally in sync — albeit decades later — with my peers. The words of old pop songs looped in my brain and when I drove back and forth from school to supermarket to community swimming pool, I tuned into the oldies' radio station for more. I went to sleep thinking of Robbie and awoke the same way. I kept checking my email, worried that he'd write, *"Can't help you anymore. Have my own work."* Or *"Kate can't handle this. Sorry."*

No emails arrived at first. Then, a week after I got home, *"Been checking the newspaper. No one's drowned. Have you figured out that the person in the waterfall is you?"*

I had figured nothing out. While part of me wanted to analyze my experiences out west, another part wanted to seal them off, much as I had sealed off my out-of-body experience with Robbie decades before. In what I would later understand as a psychological balancing act, I was trying hard to regain my equilibrium without admitting it had been disturbed.

Patrick didn't probe. Some people are completely sure of being loved and never left. I am not one of them but my husband is. He didn't seem to spend any time considering the ramifications of my week with Robbie. He believed I had gone west to work and had come back absorbed by my material, which I would now transform into a book. We rarely discussed my work in progress. He reads what I write just before it's published, and takes pride in catching typos and grammatical errors.

I'd married an engineer, to whom my work is as exotic to him as his is to me. Sometimes, he stands in the doorway of my office and watches me rearrange words and sentences on my computer screen as though writing were a mysterious thing. There's a delicate balance of distance and intimacy between us. We fit together like adjacent pieces of a puzzle, but I was 34 when we met and my husband doesn't know what my life was like before him.

Before him, my loves had been versions of Robbie: gifted, troubled, moody men with whom I lost myself to enmeshment. Patrick was highly gifted but untroubled and optimistic. Perhaps more significantly, he was French, the beneficiary of a rational, Cartesian education. I never forgot who was who.

I resumed my routines of writing every morning, then making lunch and eating it with Patrick, or going out with a friend. I organized dinners and outings with other families. As the school year drew to a close, I sewed nametapes onto my sons' clothing and sheets and, along with other grateful parents, dropped them off at their summer camps.

Patrick and I settled into the lakeside cottage I had bought when I was single. We ate when we were hungry, made love without closing the door. The days were warm and sunny, the kind you wish you could bottle up for use in winter. Yet, in September, I was glad to fly away to Prague for a break from domestic routine. I had published another book involving my family history and it had just been published in Czech.

I had begun *Where She Came From* after my mother died suddenly, of a brain aneurysm, when I was 41. I had intended to examine our complicated and fraught relationship but found that I couldn't. I chickened out and instead wrote a heavily researched, almost scholarly, history of my mother's family and her life up until the time I was born.

I had flown to Prague to promote that book, still jarred — as I had been years earlier — by hearing the intimate language of my childhood spoken by a city of strangers. This time, I was also aware of regressing to the mindset of a little girl trying to please.

My publisher had scheduled interviews, photo shoots, even an appearance on a national TV news show. For a week, I was immersed in a culture that would have been mine had it not been for a twist of history.

I posed for photographers and was struck, over and over again, by the blatant sexuality of life in Prague. My cousin, whose family lived outside the city, gave me a key to his apartment and invited me to invite anyone I wished for the night. A reporter who must have been half my age, proposed we go to bed after we completed our interview and persisted when I demurred.

I felt like an American. I heard my mother's voice mocking Puritans. Even my Prague friends, most of them my age, seemed blasé and worldly in comparison to me. By the last day, I was happy to fly home.

A presidential campaign was in full swing when I got back to Massachusetts, with both candidates campaigning in the shadow of the current President's penis and affair with a White House intern.

I had voted for President Clinton and was dismayed to find myself allied with religious fundamentalists and social conservatives arguing that he had abused his power. Good friends defended him, listing powerful men in every era and culture who helped themselves to sex and asked why I was so upset.

One reason was that my sons, aged 12 and 15, were now hearing blowjob jokes. Other mothers said jokes were the least of it. Middle school girls were giving boys blowjobs in school bathrooms and claiming that it wasn't sex.

Patrick had little patience for the jokes or the politicians or the media that kept the story vivid. But Robbie, with whom I had resumed regular contact, was interested in all of it. He noted that my mother would not have been shocked by Clinton. She was jaded about sex. Cynical.

"This book of yours isn't about you and me," he said. "I'm just a stand-in. However much you don't want to write another book about your mother, you have to. You aren't done."

He was right. At 52, I hadn't come to terms with either Robbie or my mother.

"Wasn't she a big topic in your analysis?" Robbie asked.

"Of course she was." Dimly, I had suspected that she and her *salon* of unhappy customers shaped my ambivalence about marriage.

The day before I was to have my first psychoanalytic session was a Sunday, I reminded Robbie, and Franci had invited me to lunch and a concert at Lincoln Center. She was already seated in the café when I arrived, cigarette in hand. When I leaned over to kiss her, she said, "I'm going to save you a lot of time."

I was accustomed to my mother's brusque greetings, but this was unusual even for her.

"You'll stop talking to me very soon," she said. "I was in analysis. I know. So I'll tell you now. I had an affair with Ivan."

"Who's Ivan?" Robbie asked.

"My nanny's husband." I told him. "I had a Czech nanny named Milena. Her husband's name was Ivan."

"Did you know Ivan was sleeping with your mother?"

"I don't know what I knew."

I'm going to save you a lot of time, Franci began, then told me that I had been three when I discovered her affair with Ivan. I had the chicken pox and was in bed with a fever. She and Ivan were sitting at the foot of my bed when I said, "You two look like you're married."

I told her I had no recollection of that.

How about when I was six or seven? Franci told me that when I was riding my bike in the park, I ran into her and Ivan holding hands.

I didn't remember that either, but when she asked if I remembered breaking my arm in second grade, I felt that sensation of falling.

I had fallen off a curb on Amsterdam Avenue on my way home for lunch with friends. I remembered an overpowering nausea and a white plaster cast that set my arm in a right angle and extended from my wrist almost to my shoulder. My classmates autographed it in many colors of ink.

"Ivan and I were on our way to Cape Cod, the only time we were able to get away together."

I didn't think I ever knew that but was too stunned by my mother's cascading revelations to wonder: who picked me up? who called the doctor? who took me to the hospital to have the fractured arm set in a cast? I could see that cast and the autographs in varying colors of ink that almost everyone in my class had left on it. It hadn't occurred to me to ask who had called my home to tell my parents, or where my father was.

It also hadn't occurred to me to tell my mother to shut up, that I didn't want to hear this the day before I was to start *my* psychoanalysis. As far as back as I could remember, it had been my job to listen to her. At 31, I was still doing it.

"What did you feel?" Robbie asked.

"Angry," I said. But not about her betrayal of my father. Or her betrayal of me. About the *timing* of her disclosure. And I felt angry because I felt unable to tell my mother I was angry. The blank check for behavior after the war gave her permission to do anything she needed or wanted to do.

"Why do you think she told you?" Robbie asked.

"Maybe she really was trying to save me time and money. Maybe she felt guilty. Who knows what she was doing?" I shouted into the telephone. But the analysis was supposed to be *mine.* Ivan had not been on my agenda. I disliked him as much as I loved my nanny Milena. He drank. He had oily hair and thin wet lips. At intermissions, he'd lean over and try to kiss me on my mouth. That was probably the reason I hated wet kisses.

"I remember you didn't like being kissed on the mouth," Robbie's voice broke in. "I thought maybe it was my beard you didn't like but no other girl complained. Then I thought maybe it was some Czech thing. You seemed to like everything else. Except you said you felt nothing in your breasts. Did that get straightened out?"

What? He was more interested in me than in my mother? Nobody else talked to me the way Robbie did. How could he remember details about my body that I myself had forgotten?

"It got straightened out," I replied. Years of good sex, pregnancy, childbirth, then breast-feeding had cleared out the blockage between nipples and lips and lit up the erotic circuit board. But I still disliked being kissed on the mouth, particularly by determined strangers. I didn't like being photographed either.

"Photographs?" Robbie asked.

Ivan was a radio broadcaster for Radio Free Europe but also an avid photographer, rarely without his camera. He took hundreds of photographs of my mother and me, and pasted them into scrapbooks like the Surrealists of the 1930s. He glued typed captions under the photographs, alongside Disney cartoons and magazine illustrations. The first album he made for me was titled *"Naše Helenka"* or "Our little Helen." At the end, he pasted his photograph with the caption: "Grandfather Ivan, Author."

"So he was the Anti-Kurt."

I could barely hear Robbie by then, remembering Ivan's old-fashioned camera with its large flashbulb. My mother's taste in men had been shaped by Hollywood sensation Rudolf Valentino. Her first husband who had been murdered in the war, like Ivan, had dark, straight, slicked-back hair and a haughty stance. Ivan was a hero in her eyes and also a concert buff who knew all the Czech musicians who played in New York. He was also an artisan who had made the lamp in our living room from driftwood he found on the beach. He made a series of lamps with thick cord wound around their shafts. He finished them off with glossy shellac.

I was glad I had written my mother's disclosure down the day she made it, I told Robbie. Some of the things she had said or done were so extreme that I wasn't always sure they had actually happened.

"Example?"

"This may not seem like a big deal. I had an old raincoat I loved and she hated. It was shabby. Maybe it reminded her of the war. She kept threatening to throw it out. Then one day when I opened my closet, I saw it was hanging there in shreds: she had cut it up with her pinking shears."

Robbie kept silent.

"I couldn't believe she had done it, let alone left it there for me to find. There was no way to fix it. It was destroyed. I don't remember if I cried, if I told anyone, if I confronted her. Nothing."

The feelings I had about my shredded raincoat seemed stronger in that moment than my mother's affair with Ivan.

I wondered aloud to Robbie if I should abandon my project. My memory was obviously unreliable, so what was the point of trying to write a memoir? Many people wanted to go back in time and figure out what went on with their first love. But there were good reasons most didn't. Not only was it disruptive, confusing, painful. You didn't know where it could lead. I must have sensed that something I didn't want to tackle was looming ahead of me like bad weather.

Robbie didn't argue, but suggested that I back away for a bit, try to write some *études* on themes related to my work, rather than work on the memoir itself "Don't censor yourself," he said. "Write whatever comes to mind. Let yourself be lyrical, even — forgive the word — sentimental."

Lyrical? I took him to mean I should not be afraid to sing out and, because he was Robbie, I took his cue.

~ 15 ~

I called my first *étude "Writers, Privacy, and Boundaries."* A friend in Prague had told me he stopped writing because he didn't want to go on hurting people he loved. "It wasn't worth it," he said. Was it worth it to me? Composers can write without betraying the identities of people they are writing about, I reminded Robbie. Authors confront the sticky issue of privacy.

"In journalism school, we were taught rules — that there's a contract between reporter and source. The celebrity talks to the reporter in exchange for publicity. The whistle blower trades a secret for a higher good. The source gets coverage; the reporter gets a story. The source agrees to tell the truth; the reporter agrees to separate material for publication and material that is 'off the record.' Both pledge not to make things up.

"I'm writing memoir — a hybrid form with no accountability and few rules. How do I know fact from fantasy when I'm the sole source? Some writers say they're writing strictly what they remember; some that they see no clear boundary between fact and fiction; some lie outright and tell the reader; others admit to bending or embroidering on the truth. When truth depends on memory, I have many questions.

"There's also the question of boundaries: all lives involve other people and my story involves yours. Do I have a right to tell it? What's private? What's public? Who decides?

"For years I was unable to feel separate from my mother and I transferred that pattern of relationship to all the people I loved.

In some ways that was great. There's nothing as exciting as the great merge. I shared everything I had with my mother and that sharing interfered with all my relationships until I went into analysis and found another model for intimacy. Then I finally met and married a person different enough from me that I never get confused about who's who."

As I wrote my *étude,* I could feel myself falling back into that confusion.

"There's a power issue between us here: I'm the writer and the writer controls the story. But I feel guilty about that and not entirely in control. I have a kind of amnesia about huge chunks of it and need you to be my memory. Why do I remember so little? And why do I worry so much whether you'll hang in there till the end?

"Real writers create real upheavals — in everyone, not only themselves. I've chosen to do it. But I worry about your understanding what it will mean for you to be involved in this book. I haven't thought through the possible hazards or even where I'll eventually end up. Maybe this all sounds naïve to you or you have thought it through or you take it for granted in the artistic enterprise. But you've never said it out loud. You've agreed to do something that neither you or I fully understand and that makes me nervous."

I thought I had done something momentous in sending this *étude* to Robbie. I sang out a warning for my audience of one, but Robbie replied there was no need: "I read this twice. Thought it sounded like a little prayer ceremony before you set off. I'm fine. I know this stuff."

I felt a surge of gratitude. More than needing Robbie as an archive, I needed him as a listener. He was listening intently and sometimes I thought he understood more about what I was writing than I did. I was flailing, lurching ahead without knowing where. He was telling me not to worry, to keep going. I didn't note the paradox of relying on the most erratic person I knew.

I wrote a second *étude* and called it *"Language."*

"This one feels scary to me. As a child, I loved reading books over and over again because they were so RELIABLE as well as beautiful and interesting. No matter what was going on outside or inside me, they remained the same. Reading was my anchor as well as a way of understanding events in my life that I wasn't able to process alone — and here I get weepy."

Something new had begun as I sat down to write every morning: my eyes began to tear. I wondered if I had developed a new allergy or if I was spending too much time at the screen. It didn't occur to me that I was weeping.

"Spoken language feels unstable to me. I speak four languages and feel like a person in each. My first language was Czech, and speaking it makes me regress. After I've been in Prague for a few days and come back home to Massachusetts, I feel like I'm re-entering earth from outer space.

"My father spoke no English when I was a child and neither did my nanny Milena. I had started talking early and was chattering away when I was enrolled in nursery school. The practice in the 1950s was to deposit the child and leave. No one spoke Czech of course and it must have been a terrifying experience. When I took my own kids to nursery school, I saw that some children were clearly anxious while others were not. My mother said I loved nursery school and although I cried the whole first day, I was fine. Sound familiar? Do we know what really went on?

"At age three, I began negotiating the world in English but continued in Czech at home. My younger brother refused to speak Czech and when he began school my parents realized that if they didn't want to raise a mute, they'd have to start speaking English at home. I was almost nine then and friends say I spoke English with an accent. I also had deficits in my vocabulary. I didn't know the names of important flowers or trees or animals or shades of feeling. And most embarrassing — I had no vocabulary for swearing. I couldn't tell when my parents used foul language in Czech and except when my mother called a difficult customer a bitch, cursing was not part of my life. Public

discourse was sanitized in the 1950s — it was rare to hear anyone swear on TV or in the movies.

"But the word 'Fuck!' was carved into our elevator and desks at school, and scrawled on the walls of many toilet stalls. I was ashamed of not knowing what it meant and too embarrassed to ask. I was used to being a smart kid and didn't like being in the position of not knowing what everyone else knew.

"Guess what strategy I came up with? I pretended I was a TV reporter, holding a pretend microphone and interviewing my classmates: 'So what do you think the word fuck means?' This was embarrassing to me then and painful to remember now, though it seems a psychologically brilliant and even charming way to solve a pressing problem as a 10-year-old. It makes me weep. Maybe because I see how out of it I was, maybe because in some way, I still am.

"When we were teenagers, you told me I didn't talk like anybody else you knew. Maybe this is part of why. Words aren't straightforward for me. A word can feel 'wrong' to me, like a wrong note. But the right word often doesn't come to me and I swim around in very murky waters trying to find it. That murkiness gets murkier when it comes to anything involving love or sex.

"But on to what I started out thinking this essay would really be about: obscene language, cursing, swearing. I'll get rid of the feminist stuff first, because it's easy and it's been said by so many women so many times that it's boring. I feel swearing as an assault — not some theoretical social or moral issue, but an immediate, concrete, tangible, thing like a slap in the face. I don't like the word bitch. I hate the word cunt."

I didn't realize how agitated I was becoming as I wrote my *étude,* let alone why. Or that Robbie had been the one person in my adolescent life who swore.

"Part of my dislike of swearing comes from feeling coerced: that sophistication requires me as an adult to use this language and buy into its assumptions. If I refuse, I'm dismissed as a prude, someone who thinks herself 'better than,' or irremediably

'middle-class.' I remember how in the Sixties, obscenity was de rigueur, *a repudiation of established norms, considered more authentic than polite speech — the way that working-class people were considered more 'real' than the middle-class. Cursing was a form of bonding, especially between men. At chorus, you used to curse and trade dirty jokes with your pals while I waited for you to drive me home.*

"Those jokes set off all kinds of alarms in me — and that you of all people were telling them! I couldn't complain, not to you or anyone else. I didn't want to seem more naïve than I already felt. But I wondered about dirty jokes and the way people use the word 'fuck,' to express anger. I'm acculturated now: I've learned to yell 'fucking asshole!' when a driver cuts me off on the highway, but still hate the joke that you and Bill would tell in rehearsal: what are the three big lies? I love you; the check is in the mail; and I won't come in your mouth. It was completely inappropriate for you to be saying that in front of me when I was fifteen. I'm not in the business of giving out prizes for speech but I am in the business of keeping my sanity and for whatever reasons it unhinges me."

I was so absorbed by my *étude* that after I sent it to Robbie, I was startled by his response.

"That's some judgment on a 19-year-old," he wrote back. *"I feel like I'm abandoning you — which I said I would not — but I don't have the energy to keep going. Seems you have the stuff you need from me. I don't remember any more... We've stumbled into some area I don't understand and I need my psychic space back.*

"So let's stop. At least that is what I really want to do."

I saw abandoned girls. Tiger Lily bound to a rock with the water rising and Peter Pan nowhere in sight. Dorothy imprisoned in the fortress of the Wicked Witch. Why had I ever thought I could depend on Robbie?

I was waking up two or three times a night by then, and weeping at my desk every morning. There was no feeling attached and no sound. When I tried to write about what was happening in my journal, my right hand trembled so much that I could barely read my own handwriting.

The strangest thing was that I felt a need to keep what was happening a secret. It took weeks before I focused on the tears leaking from my eyes. I ignored the obvious — that they had to do with what I was writing — and theorized about menopause and mid-life. I was 53. It was winter, between Thanksgiving and Christmas. Everyone was stressed out.

None of my three guys noticed.

I had never understood how political wives managed to hide their alcoholism or addiction from their families for decades. Now, I did. If I was present, showed up on schedule, and was responsive in conversation, no one suspected anything. Only our dog knew. He began coming close to my desk as I worked and resting his head against my thigh.

Tears connote grief, I told myself, after I gave a reading during which I started weeping onstage. I hid that too. But I finally forced myself to do the closest thing I knew to asking for help. *"In the interests of full disclosure,"* I emailed Robbie. *"I should tell you I've been weeping. No noise. Just a steady seepage of tears."*

~ 16 ~

Robbie returned to his role of collaborator and coach. From 3,000 miles away, he diagnosed my weeping as an overdue expression of long-suppressed grief. "It's time," he said. "I knew that this book would bring you to it."

I had no such idea. I had embarked on a memoir of my adolescence with my first love thinking that it would be easy, even a lark. I had no consciousness yet of what I was trying to write about, but I knew I needed to take time out. Since schools would be closed for a long weekend and my sons loved to ski while my spouse did not, I offered to take them to a lodge in Stowe, Vermont.

Stowe was not a casual choice; it had been my family's favorite getaway in the 1950s. Stowe was like a Central European village then, filled with refugees who skied like my parents and the Baron von Trapp's family whose escape from the Nazis was then being made into *The Sound of Music.*

It was dark outside when my father strapped our heavy wooden skis to the ski rack and we loaded the car. It took ten hours to drive from the Upper West Side to Stowe in those pre-interstate days, and dark again when we unloaded and sat down to a hearty Czech dinner. For a few days, my parents were on vacation.

Fifty years later, Stowe was a popular resort and an easy drive from our Massachusetts home. Patrick was grateful for the time to work uninterrupted. I didn't tell him that I would be working too, trying to tune into what the book I was writing had stirred up in my mind.

We started north on the interstate at 6 a.m. The sun was not yet up, the road was clear of snow, and I set the cruise control at 75. My sons had thrown their skis, poles, boots and parkas into the mini-van and gone back to sleep. My husband had filled up the gas tank. There was no traffic. I had at least three hours in which to pay attention to my thoughts.

My mother was a passionate skier. The sport was not a luxury but life to her and, like so many things, had to do with the war. She had been eighteen, on her first ski vacation alone in the Alps, when her father suddenly called her home to Prague. The next day, Hitler sent troops into Austria. That marked the beginning of the war for my mother. The end, too, was marked by skiing. My mother had returned home from the concentration camps, deeply depressed. On the last day of 1945, only the intervention of a policeman had stopped her from throwing herself into Prague's river.

He had walked her to the rented room where she was staying. The next day, as my mother told it, she chose to live. She borrowed a pair of skis and took the train to the mountains where she had skied as a girl and, after arriving in New York, even when they couldn't pay the butcher, she took us to Stowe. My brother Tommy and I were enrolled in ski class while she skied from the moment the lifts opened until they closed, whatever the condition of the snow or the weather.

My father was not a good skier. You could easily spot his figure on the bunny slope as he made his slow turns, as though he were sitting in a chair. He had learned on his honeymoon, to please my mother.

I was neither a good nor passionate skier. When the snow was soft and it was warm and sunny, I sometimes enjoyed it but I was often miserable in Stowe where it was icy and cold. I got frostbite and didn't like the speed of flying down the mountain, with the possibility of losing control and getting hurt if I skidded on an ice patch and hit a rock or tree. I was very cautious, almost as rigid as my father. I fell a lot and complained that I wanted to stop.

Lift tickets — not to speak of gas and food and lodging — were an extravagance for our family. We skied unless it was hailing or so windy that the lifts shut down. Franci skied with Tommy and me in the afternoons, practicing what we had learned in the mornings. We skied until the light and snow merged into an indefinite gray, the air was bitter cold, and whatever pleasure I felt had faded. I had stopped skiing after I started psychoanalysis but Tommy became a certified ski instructor. I glanced in my rear-view mirror, noted that both my sons loved to ski and here we were driving north, repeating, repeating.

By the time we crossed from Massachusetts into Vermont, my eyes were wet again and I realized that I was in an altered state of mind. Words and images were coming at me like bats at night, colliding and making my chest tighten. My consciousness seemed to have broken away from its usual tracks. The sensation was like sexual arousal but there was no erotic organ I could connect it to. I didn't like how far from my body I felt and how fast my mind was racing. I tried to focus on the landscape to slow it down, registering the silhouettes of bare trees, the snowfields, the occasional house or barn. I was searching for a radio station when someone asked for a pit stop.

I pulled off at the next exit, noting how everything was easier for me than it had been for my mother. I hadn't had to pack a hamper of food; we could buy anything we needed. My husband had a good job. We slept in a queen-sized bed in a real bedroom. Our car was kept in our garage, not on the street. When we set off again on the interstate, my sons chose a movie to watch on their laptop. My time was my own and I tuned back into the unusual monologue in my mind.

Robbie had said that the person in the waterfall was me and he was right. The scariest part — drowning in the torrent of water — was behind me. Now, I was just swimming underwater and I knew how to do that. I swam nearly every day. My father always said that anything that happened looked better after a swim. That calmed me down and by the time I reached the exit to Stowe, I could focus on getting my boys to the mountain. I unloaded them, gave them lunch and lift money, and watched until they were aboard the gondola. Then I drove to our lodge, checked in and settled into my small room.

In my 20s, I had taken an extraordinary mescaline trip with a group of friends. Soon after I swallowed the drug, I was convinced I had become a small planet hurtling out into space. The friend who was monitoring us instructed me to lie down on a couch and told the three others to sit on me. Their weight brought my consciousness back into my body, but it had escaped again — as it had the first time I slept with Robbie.

I hadn't yet read much psychology and didn't know that the term *autoscopy* had been coined to describe this kind of dissociative experience. I hadn't heard of the concept of dissociation as a defense against overwhelming feelings.

I lay down on the single bed, tripping without a drug, trying to observe the kaleidoscope of visual and verbal forms, turning toward them the way good drivers turn into a skid.

I had been sixteen when I had the first autoscopic experience that I remembered, singing on the stage of Manhattan's Town Hall. Robbie had been there then too, standing on a riser behind me. Mr. Labovitz, wearing a tuxedo, was conducting a concert version of *The Magic Flute,* which I had seen several times with my mother at the Met. It featured an abducted girl, a powerful and jealous mother, an absent father, a lecherous servant, and a hero who walked through fire and water to save her.

Somewhere in the last chorus, my consciousness flew out of my mouth and up toward the ceiling. From there in the dark, I saw myself and the entire chorus, and Mr. Labovitz conducting us. I had flown out in a kind of whooosh! And after a while I was sucked back in a kind of whoosh! It was so strange, so uncanny. I didn't tell anyone about it, not even Robbie. I thought maybe that I wasn't breathing properly and had passed out for a few seconds. But if I had passed out, I would have fallen. I hadn't. My body just kept standing there and singing and I was outside of it. Like the time I left my body when I slept with Robbie. What was the connection? I had no clue.

I had brought a book by V.S. Naipaul to the ski lodge. Now, a sentence leaped out: *"However creatively one travels, however deep an experience in childhood or middle-age, it takes thought (a sifting of impulses, ideas and references that become more multifarious as one grows older) to understand what one has lived through or where one has been."*

The thought seemed both obvious and ingenious to me.

When the alarm I had set rang, I snapped back into my role as mother, driving up to the mountain, collecting my children, asking appropriate questions about the state of the trails, the length of the lift lines, what they had for lunch. I chatted reasonably all through dinner, after which they played ping-pong and watched TV while I fell into a dreamless sleep.

The next morning I drove my kids back to the mountain, then put on my cross-country skis and took off along a stream. The morning air was clear and cold; the white fields sparkled in the sunlight, with drifts three and four feet high in some places. Snow covered most of the stones in the stream but you could see a few through the clear running water, gray-greens, gray-blues. My father taught me to swim before I could walk and I recalled what he said about the ocean. I shouldn't be scared of the waves. I should dive under them to where the water was calm.

I passed no one as I slid silently along on my skis. I stopped every now and then, not because I was tired but because in this odd water language in which I was thinking, it was important to note how the water pooled and understand that it gathered into places where you could look into it and see what was underneath. *The Sound of Music* played in my mind. Raindrops, roses, mountains, streams. A boy who was older and wiser, teaching the girl what to do. Kitschy Broadway lyrics, but comforting in their rhymes.

I decided to drive to the Trapp Family lodge. I had last been there as a child and remembered candles and bells — sleigh bells, cow bells, porcelain dinner bells on delicate ribbons. I was in search of a postcard of the snow-covered stream. The place was still crammed with bells and varieties of maple sugar candy but no postcard of a stream.

I got back into my van and drove to an art gallery. There, I found a large, black-and-white framed photograph of a sun-lit, snow-covered stream. Robbie and Kate had just bought their first house. I had it sent to them as a housewarming gift.

~ 17 ~

Back home, I told Patrick about Stowe but not about what had transpired inside me. I knew it would alarm him. My engineer spouse likes to identify problems and fix them. He's uncomfortable with ambiguity and designs scenarios rather than embarking on the long, often fruitless quest of creative process. The man who flourished in that kind of work was Robbie. I emailed him that he would be receiving a package from Stowe and about my trip along the stream.

It came as a surprise when he replied, *"I'm a little worried about you. You have to be able to slow down your brain. And if you get to a place where you can't, you should let me know. Then we can both feel that everything is under control."*

I assured him that everything was under control, though I knew, by those first months of 2001, that it was not. Digging into the past had jarred loose many disturbing memories. Instead of identifying and examining them, however, I became obsessed with losing Robbie. I worried when there was no message from him and worried what the subtext was when there was. I reread what he wrote to make sure I understood it. I needed help but carried on as though I didn't.

I had speaking engagements in New York and in Virginia. At the first venue, a conference of museum educators, I read my speech as though it were in a foreign language and heard my voice catch while answering questions. At the airport, I noticed myself rereading my boarding pass over and over again. I found it impossible to remember my flight number, departure time, and gate. I boarded and deplaned, fastened and unfastened my seatbelt as if in a trance. I smiled at the women who met me at the airport in Virginia and, when they took me to an old-fashioned B & B, told them that I wished to rest.

There was a museum across the street and, for the better part of an hour, I sat on its floor staring at a large Rothko canvas, trying to drink in something of its serenity. Images of my own creation kept displacing the ones before me. I saw myself standing on two chairs. Someone was slowly pulling them apart; my legs were sliding away from under me; my body was going to split in half.

I returned to my room and looked for a book to escape into but found only tourist magazines and a guide titled *Norfolk: Historic Southern Port.* I could barely make sense of more than a paragraph at a time but one sentence seemed so significant to me that I copied it down: *"The impropriety of writing critically of living persons makes writing contemporary history exceedingly difficult."* Not to speak of memoir, I added. It seemed too hard to try to think through why.

That evening, it took all my concentration to read and speak intelligibly and answer questions about my work. I managed to hold myself together until I got back into my room and into the large four-poster bed, where I lay thinking about Lot's wife, who was turned into a pillar of salt when she disregarded a warning not to look back at Sodom and did. Delving into the past was a treacherous undertaking. Instead of choosing what I wished to revisit, I was being visited by states of mind so intense I was incapable of articulating them, almost incapable of getting back on the airplane and flying home.

Patrick met me at the airport and, once again, it was important to me to conceal my agitation, to behave as though nothing were amiss. My talks had gone well, I said, but I was exhausted and needed to sleep. After catching up with the boys, I checked my computer and found a message from Robbie. "At the risk of getting you mad, I want to say that to be safe you need to find a therapist who has experience with creative people. I'm sure you've been having some kind of mania — a normal thing for many artists, but if not dealt with can become dangerous. Please..."

The next morning, alone in my office, I flipped through my phonebook, looking for a New York City number I hadn't dialed in years. I reached a friendly woman's voice, identified myself as a patient from 20 years earlier and asked whether Dr. M. still practiced psychoanalysis.

He did a bit of everything, she replied. Child psychiatry. Psychopharm. Consulting. Psychoanalysis.

Did he ever work over the phone? I asked.

Sure, she said. Would I like to leave a message?

~ 18 ~

For almost two decades, I'd sent my psychoanalyst New Year's cards as though they were deposits to a bank. Each card featured a color photograph of me and my growing family — evidence, I thought, of a successful therapy. That January of 2001, I felt it was time to draw on my investment.

Dr. M. called back and asked, "What's going on?"

I told him I wasn't sure. He conducted a physical exam via telephone. He asked: was I breathing normally? Any changes in my appetite? Apart from the weeping at my computer and while speaking in public, did I feel depressed? Was I moving around a lot or sitting still?

I wasn't moving around. My appetite was normal. I didn't feel depressed, but I was weeping when I sat down to write and when I spoke in public. My sleep had become so disturbed that I had started using anti-histamines or sedatives left over from various family ailments.

Why didn't I want to see a local therapist?

I didn't want to educate a new shrink about my background or my parents' war. I didn't want to drive home agitated after sessions. Then, I heard myself say, "And I want a child psychiatrist."

That was a surprise. Until his assistant told me he saw kids, I hadn't known that Dr. M. *was* a child psychiatrist.

He waited for me to say more. I didn't. I was taking in the sounds of buses, trucks, and ambulances on the avenue below his windows in Manhattan, the soundtrack of my childhood.

We scheduled a phone session.

Unlike many people, I had grown up largely oblivious to my inner life. Unless I had a nightmare, I rarely paid attention to my dreams. I was as unconscious of daydreaming as I was of fantasy. Riding the subway in Manhattan, I sometimes imagined my train speeding to Auschwitz, but didn't formulate that vision as a "fantasy" until a psychologist told me.

I had researched and written my first book about children of survivors in what I now can identify as a dissociated state. It had felt like driving through a blizzard to me. I couldn't see ahead or behind me — nothing but the page I was working on. Sitting at my typewriter, I blocked out the meaning of my narrative as I created it, focused on each word and sentence. It was only after I read my book, and took in the whole of what I'd written, that I decided to seek out psychotherapy.

My grandmother had undertaken the talking cure near Vienna in 1908; my mother, in Manhattan of the 1950s. Psychoanalysis seemed like a family tradition. I consulted an analytic elder who asked me two questions: what was my goal? What kind of person did I imagine as my ideal analyst?

I told the consultant that I wanted to redo my childhood with a different mother: someone smart, cultured, Jewish and Czech like Franci, but with a key difference — no concentration camp. Of course, I understood that finding someone like that was unlikely.

I was sent to Marianne Young, a Park Avenue analyst about my mother's age who told me, before she died, that she had sailed out of Europe on the last passenger ship. It had been torpedoed; she had survived on a lifeboat, married and had a daughter who died. She had long wished for a young female analysand who spoke Czech. But during my on-the-couch, three-times-a-week, classical psychoanalysis, Dr. Young revealed nothing but an accent that resembled my mother's.

When we met for the first time in her formal apartment, Dr. Young instructed me to be prompt. Sessions would be 50 minutes with time subtracted for lateness. If I missed a session, I would pay for it — without exception. This was no California free-for-all, I remember thinking, but a time-tested Central European rite. Sitting silently in her funereal waiting room, sometimes I thought all that was missing were the candelabra and the robes.

Did I have any concerns before we began? I said that I worried about whether analysis might end my urge to write and force me to fit into some theoretical paradigm. Dr. Young replied that forcing patients would not be treating them as human beings. I lay down on her black leather couch and she instructed me to say whatever came to mind, without self-censoring.

I found psychoanalysis difficult. I was a journalist, accustomed to training my eyes and ears outward, not inward. By temperament too, I was an extrovert and, in addition, my parents had encouraged activity, not introspection. I was more accustomed to banishing than paying attention to what came to mind and felt inept at following her instruction. Dr. Young sat on a chair behind the couch and rarely spoke. Without seeing her, I couldn't guess what she wanted me to say.

Many — perhaps most — 21st century psychologists view psychoanalysis as obsolete, but I found it spectacularly useful. For what seemed the first time in my life, I discovered that I had an inner life. I began to recognize and name states of mind, particularly confusion and ambivalence. I relished saying the words, "I don't know" and "I'm not sure." Analysis felt like the first thing in my life that was all mine. No parents, no lovers, no friends in there — just me. At the end of a year, I felt so much transition that I made a drawing of myself moving from one body into another. I felt that so much had changed that I asked Dr. Young for a break to catch up with myself.

When I returned, Dr. Young said my hours had been filled. I wondered if there was more to it, but do not remember any strong feelings about leaving her and being referred to Dr. M.

Dr. M. shared a busy waiting room with other doctors, their names engraved on a brass plate beside the outside door. He wore a three-piece suit that made him look like the banker father in *Mary Poppins* even though his hair was longish, like Robbie's. He was tall, slightly awkward, and didn't sound like a New Yorker. I assumed that he had grown up far away.

I sat down and, since I was by then accustomed to saying what came to mind, I told him I was a journalist who had written a book about intergenerational transmission of trauma and taught at New York University. I lived by an academic calendar, traveled to give readings and might have to miss some sessions. Unlike Dr. Young, he said nothing about paying for missed sessions, just asked me to give him a two-week heads up. Despite his suit, he seemed so unlike me and unlike Dr. Young that I decided he needed some background.

I gave him a summary of my book: the war; the refugee community; how difficult it was to separate from parents who equated separation with death; my father's death when I was 26; my promise to take care of my mother after he died; how my mother often felt like an albatross around my neck; how deeply I hated listening to myself whine about this laundry list of complaints.

Dr. M. had startled me with a chuckle.

That might have ended someone else's therapy, but it jump-started mine. Wherever he came from, I thought, Dr. M. had a sense of humor. But when I entered his office next time and he gestured toward his couch, I balked. I sat down in a chair. Dr. M. did too. Despite his height and formal attire, he didn't strike me as even a tad threatening, so when he asked what came to mind, I had no trouble replying: green straps across my chest, hospital bed. Tonsillectomy at age three and a half. Wow! Why hadn't I remembered that with Dr. Young?

I made up my mind to lie down on the couch, very pleased with myself and my new analyst.

~ 19 ~

That spring of 1981, I was up for tenure, the first woman in my department to undergo this always nerve-wracking process, and I was being judged by colleagues who were all men whose behavior toward me as their token woman ranged from patronizing to sexually harassing — a term not yet in use.

My elderly office mate had startled me with a proposition almost as soon as I moved in, insisting that I would benefit from his years of ghostwriting books for a prominent sexologist. He was 65 and a tenured professor; I was by far the youngest member of the department and didn't feel I could complain. Two other colleagues routinely bragged about flirting with students, but warned me not to indulge. During a departmental lunch, our Chairman told a sexual joke about Helen Keller: "How do you know when she's coming? She signs her moans." Everyone had broken up in laughter but me.

When I recounted all this to Dr. M., he didn't chuckle, and I felt emboldened to complain. I disliked my university colleagues and found the tenure process humiliating, but needed to do whatever I was asked in order to keep my job and subsidize my writing. I wished that I had as much clarity about personal matters as I did about professional ones. I rarely understood whether I or my lover had ended a relationship. At 32, I wasn't sure if I wanted to get married or not. I wasn't sure how much this had to do with my parents' marriage.

I also talked about my father's death during my first year of being a college professor. Heart attack on Saturday, funeral on Sunday and Monday, the first day of my second semester, I was teaching. By then I had learned the term dissociation. I felt nothing and experienced interactions with other people as occurring through a pane of glass. My tall athletic father had fallen to the pavement and an instant death while walking the dog on Riverside Drive; I thought of his favorite Biblical figure — Samson. Old and blind, shorn of his empowering hair, Samson leaned against two pillars of the temple where he was imprisoned and brought the roof crashing down.

Though the war had destroyed my father's religious beliefs, Kurt often read me *Bible Stories for Children* to practice his English. Until his death, I had thought of my mother as the central pillar of our family because she was the breadwinner, but it turned out that my father was the pillar.

In the weeks after his death, I had a recurrent hallucination as I walked to work: a pliers-like instrument descending from the sky, headed for my mouth. Years after my father's death, I still saw it clearly. Did it allude to my tonsillectomy, my mother surviving the war by claiming she was an electrician?

I didn't get very far trying to decipher the meaning of this image with my analyst back then, but I finally was able to grieve for my father. Visits with my widowed mother became less fraught. So did work. I was awarded tenure, with its guarantee of life-long employment. I found psychoanalysis effective and intellectually challenging. I was so committed to what I regarded as a discipline that in the spring of 1982, when I was invited to a conference in Switzerland, the prospect of missing two weeks of analysis nearly dissuaded me from accepting.

The conference, organized by the Swiss UJA in Davos turned out to be a mixer for 800 Jewish bachelors and bachelorettes living across Europe. I had been recruited, along with other authors and public figures, to provoke conversation between attendees. I was sorry I didn't qualify since I was myself, what they called a *célibataire.* And here I was running a "workshop."

Patrick was a French Jewish bachelor who chose to participate in my workshop. A tall man in a suit, he had peppered me with questions afterwards: what was my book about? Why wasn't I married? Did I want children? Our first meeting, over Viennese pastries, was more like a job interview than a casual encounter. I wondered why he was wasting time with me instead of pursuing a European *célibataire,* but I enjoyed being the center of his attention.

I noted the fair skin and pampered look of Parisian men in Renoir paintings. He described himself as a *technocrate* who worked for the French Ministry of Industry — something having to do with coal and electricity. I assumed that, apart from speaking impressive English with an engaging accent, he was likely as boring as any other company man.

But over that long weekend in Davos, I wasn't bored. We attended the lectures and social events together. Though he was 28 to my 34, he behaved as though he was older than me. He even drove me to the airport when I flew home.

When I returned to the couch, I tried to say what came to mind about my trip but I wasn't sure how to describe what had happened between Patrick and me. We had spent two long and pleasurable weekends together with no sexual overture on either side. It hadn't been until Patrick drove me to the airport and said good-bye that he had finally kissed me. I had enjoyed what I perceived as an old-fashioned courtship but it made me anxious. Maybe he was gay. Maybe he wasn't interested. I had no faith in my radar regarding men.

Instead of exploring the possible reasons why, I free-associated about inviting Patrick to visit me. My girlfriends pointed out that Paris closed down in August. He would have a month off. But, a month was a long time. What would I do if I had made a mistake? After a few sessions with my analyst, I invited Patrick to visit and he accepted.

My subsequent sessions had focused on sexual logistics. Where would I drive from the airport? My apartment had only one bed. What if I didn't want to have sex? My cottage in

Massachusetts had a guestroom. It was four hours from JFK but I decided we'd drive directly there after he landed.

August arrived. Patrick emerged from the plane into the heat wearing a suit. When I told him we were driving to Massachusetts, his only reaction was to request a map. Then he started asking about roads and bridges. He was an engineer, I remembered. What had I gotten myself into? I was no seductress and Patrick no seducer. I remembered my father's notion of a swim in cold water enhancing all things. There was a state park with a waterfall en route. Would he like to stop for a swim?

Patrick located it on his map and said, "Okay."

Mosquitoes had begun to thrum in the twilight. We undressed in the parking lot; Patrick on one side of the car, I on the other. Our hands met as we walked toward the waterfall. The mosquitoes discouraged dawdling. We jumped into the pool of cold water, splashed around, and then swam into each other's arms. By the time we got home, I'd stopped worrying where he'd sleep.

Things moved very quickly after that. In September, when Dr. M. returned from vacation and I returned to NYU, I told my analyst I was investigating taking a sabbatical in France and Patrick was investigating a job in the U.S.

Dr. M. made no comment about my plans until I said Patrick had been offered a job in Harvard Square, and I was moving to join him in Cambridge. That, in 1982, meant ending my analysis. No one then did therapy by phone. He replied that if I quit analysis again, as I had done with Dr. Young, I'd be postponing essential psychological business.

Surely he didn't expect me to put my life on hold in order to talk about it, I said.

If I didn't understand old patterns of behavior, replied my analyst, I would keep on repeating them.

I left analysis, left my job, my mother, my friends and New York City behind. I was turning the page, starting a new chapter of my life.

"I guess there's no way these things don't eventually catch up with you," I said to Dr. M. nearly two decades later, and was relieved when all I heard back over the phone was "Uh-huh."

I thought then that I needed a tune-up, maybe a couple of sessions — at most a few months. I didn't think that I was resuming a twice-deferred treatment for a long-buried trauma that would last eight years.

~ 20 ~

I sent Dr. M. my *études* and a summary of my trips at the waterfall with Robbie and in Stowe with my sons. Then I told Patrick that my writing had led me back into therapy, that I'd pay for it myself, and that I did not want to be interrogated.

I was relieved when he held back his questions. Patrick, like me, rations what he wants to know. His bottom line is: do what you need to do and where you want to do it, but come back soon and don't change too much because I love you the way you are. Psychoanalysis was associated in his French mind with art and intellect, not illness or trauma. I seemed normal to him. Better than normal. I seemed more attentive to the home front. I was as interested in sex again as during our first months of marriage, excited by his body and the erotic possibilities of my own.

All this I see only in retrospect: I was in too much turmoil to be conscious of it then, in 2001. My mind churned away as I drove to the supermarket, swam laps in our town pool, even as I tried to write. To slow down, I listened to Glenn Gould play Bach, made fires in the fireplace and soups in the kitchen, took out volume after volume of art books and stared at the organization of paintings.

It was then that Patrick announced a consulting trip to Singapore and I surprised myself by contesting its necessity. Just getting there took 24 hours. What if there was an emergency? Did he really have to go?

In fact, things were easier for me with him gone. I kept a pen and notebook beside my bed, so that I could capture dreams. They were turbulent, mixing people and places from childhood, adolescence and middle age. In one — alluding to another Bible story I read with my father — Patrick and I were sitting naked in a bathtub on a Jerusalem rooftop. Robbie was on a higher roof, gazing down at us the way King David gazed at Bathsheba before sending her husband off to war.

I don't know if I related this dream to Dr. M. I remember nothing of our second session except his giving me all his telephone numbers and instructing me to call "if necessary."

That was a shock. Dr. M. had never instructed me to do anything before.

I replaced the telephone receiver, and sat at my desk. It was mid-morning in early February, quiet, the bright winter sunlight reflecting off fresh snow. Then something even more shocking. I thought: Dr. M. must be worried about something. What's he worried about? Sexual abuse. Someone came in my mouth. Who? Ivan.

This was a bomb with no sound or smoke. Ivan: my nanny's husband, my self-appointed "grandfather," my mother's lover.

He had chased me into corners, taken photos of me, kissed me with wet lips. But sexually abused me? I didn't want to even consider it. For a long time I didn't move. Time seemed to expand and contract like the folds of an accordion.

I drove to the community center pool and swam. Then I drove back home and checked my email. From Singapore, Patrick wrote that he had been swimming too. I wrote back that we were having a blizzard.

I couldn't suppress the words that had surfaced in my mind: *What's Dr. M. worried about? Someone came in my mouth.* As I walked the dog in the snow-filled woods I began to weep again.

I remembered Ivan backing me into corners, his wet lips and wet-looking hair, the light bulbs on his camera. I recalled the sentence my sons had been taught in daycare: *It's my body and I don't want you to touch it!* I had repeated it with them with a kind of delight with the way they said it — like a Pledge of Alliance to themselves.

I had worried about them even though they were both tall and strong. When they were too old to take into the ladies' room when we traveled, I stationed myself outside the men's room and called in at intervals, "Guys! Are you OK in there?" If they didn't answer, I disregarded convention and walked in to check.

The blizzard had obscured the trails behind our house and I got lost. I followed my dog through drifts. Snow melted inside my boots. I lost all sense of orientation, had no idea where I was until finally the dog led me home.

Back in the house, I tried everything I knew to calm myself down: I made a fire. I made tea. I cut up vegetables for soup, listened to music. I didn't call anyone. Without knowing why, I felt sworn to secrecy. Above all, I felt that my situation — whatever it was — must not affect my children.

Two days later, I sent out my first cautious signal. Across the continent, to Robbie: *"My analyst gave me all his phone numbers. Maybe he thinks whatever is going on with me is dangerous but he hasn't said what."*

I couldn't write the words that had come into my mind. Instead I wrote to Robbie: *"I think: sexual abuse — a cliché but it IS about sex and language and fear that goes way back."*

"Have thought about this," Robbie emailed back. And I found that casual, concise response reassuring.

My sons and I called Singapore to sing "Happy Birthday" to Patrick over the telephone. For a few moments I enjoyed the comfort of family ritual. Then we dispersed and I was back in a whirlpool of what seemed like random associations.

I had been afraid to give birth to a daughter. I worried how I'd raise her to be free and safe. At seven — eight? — a Czech boy had kept following me and repeatedly tried to stick his hand between my thighs. I knew that was called "goosing" in English — another word I didn't understand. When I told my mother, she had not scolded him or his parents, just told me, "That's how boys are."

Had I complained to my father? Had either of them laughed about it? I don't remember complaining again.

I could not say the words, "came in my mouth" to anyone. Too brutal. Humiliating. Unbearable. And what evidence did I have that it had happened? That I didn't like kissing anyone on the mouth? That dirty jokes embarrassed me?

Since I couldn't talk to anyone about it, I went online. There, in 2001, I found two million hits for "sexual abuse."

That was one year before the *Boston Globe* broke the story of systemic sexual abuse of children by Catholic priests and the cover-up by the Church. I read media accounts of the sexual molestation scandals of children in daycare centers in the 1980s. The most sensational had occurred on the West Coast and I hadn't followed the news stories at the time. They described widespread hysteria, satanic cults, and a witch-hunt against the accused. Misguided police officers, medical personnel and therapists had led the children into giving false testimony. It seemed to me that the reality of molestation and its effect on the children drew far less attention from the media than the "falsely-accused" adults.

Another group of items that came up online had to do with adult women who had retrospectively reported sexual abuse by a family member. Their accounts were disparaged by a "False Memory Syndrome Foundation" and its supporters. They questioned the motivations and even the sanity of the plaintiffs and also accused malevolent therapists of "implanting" false memories into the minds of their clients. One expert claimed that never, in all of recorded literature, had there been a case of sexual abuse that had been forgotten and later remembered.

Some experts argued that individuals traumatized as children could react with partial or complete amnesia for the trauma for a time, then recover accurate memories — by themselves or in psychotherapy. Others argued that recovered memories of abuse were partly or fully fictitious.

I didn't want any part of this war. We still had a bookstore in town then. I drove to it and on a shelf marked "Health" found the classic text: *The Courage to Heal: A Guide for Women Survivors of Sexual Abuse.* Sitting on the floor, I sped through its 600 pages. Sexual abuse had been documented in one out of three girls and one out of seven boys. No nationality, social class, or religious group was exempt. Nothing slowed me down until I reached a paragraph that described what had happened to me the first time I slept with Robbie. "At its most extreme," I read, "you literally leave your body. This feat, which some yogis work for decades to achieve, comes naturally to children during severe trauma... Many adult survivors still do this when they feel scared."

I closed the book, stood up, and replaced it. I didn't want any reminders of my preoccupation in my home. But when I got home, I found a message from Dr. M.

"I was not comfortable with the way our last session ended," I read, *"and wondered subsequently if waiting until Thursday was too long. So I tried to call but since there was no answer I decided to write you this note instead. How are you doing?"*

All my careful defenses fell away.

How was I doing? Part of me was giving a very good performance of wife and mother. Part of me was wondering whether I had fabricated a false memory of sexual abuse. Part of me was floating up into the air like the balloons in New York's annual Thanksgiving Day Parade, tethered to earth by my sons, and Dr. M. himself.

I'm not waving; I'm drowning — a line of poetry came to mind as I pondered a response to Dr. M. Instead I wrote, *"It's nice of you to email. You're right: a lot happened since our last session and it started as soon as we hung up."*

Then I tried to reassure *him: "I've been researching sexual abuse and on a scale of 1-10, think my own experience was a 3. Things are under control, but if you have an opening before our next scheduled session, I'd be interested to get going on this."*

~ 21 ~

There was no going back but I didn't go forward at first. I didn't speak the words *someone came in my mouth* and, unlike the "malevolent therapists" described online, mine kept silent as I cross-examined myself out loud: could this have happened? Where? When? How could I — a reporter — have succeeded for years in repressing it? How could I be sure it wasn't a fantasy?

For months, Dr. M. listened and I found that reassuring. It allowed me to react to my own words rather than to his and it gave me a sense of safety. Though I was in distress, I wasn't drowning and felt in full view of a lifeguard. But I forgot much of what I said in session and was unable, afterwards, to summarize its content. As a reporter, I took for granted my ability to do these things and used a tape recorder to back-up my memory. In therapy, I had no back-up.

Had Dr. M. actually said, "You're not going to remember this"? Or was that my invention? I had started, out loud, the sentence: Men like blowjobs; you are a man; therefore... and then I had stopped. Therefore what? My mind went blank, my mouth closed. It would be eight years before I could complete that sentence. Had Dr. M. pressed me to continue then, I might have hung up the phone. I was infinitely grateful to be talking to him long-distance. I wanted him to be alert, responsive but far away — like a NASA engineer at ground control, who knew what to do when astronauts lost the ability to communicate.

During those first months of what I cautiously called recovered memory, holding onto Patrick grounded me. His physical presence had a calming effect on me in a way not dissimilar from my father's. When we walked, we held hands; at night, we slept like stacked spoons. Dr. M. didn't ask me how the physical or sexual intimacy in my marriage was faring and I didn't tell him. I went silent whenever what came to mind was remotely erotic and detoured around any term that alluded to sex. A word like "rectify" stopped me short by its proximity to the word "erect." In order to avoid it, I shut off whole networks of association.

If I remembered that I had self-censored, I berated myself. How could Dr. M. do his job if I didn't do mine? Yet, when he asked, "Did you have another thought?" I often said, "No," knowing that I did.

It was almost two months before I could travel to Manhattan and actually see Dr. M. He had moved his office to an upper floor of a building in Manhattan's priciest zip code. The lobby seemed small to me, the elevator claustrophobic, the corridor dim and narrow. His waiting room was cold, and empty — nothing like the bustling waiting room I remembered.

After a few moments, Dr. M. opened the door. I wouldn't have recognized him if I had passed him in the street. He was still tall and still wearing a suit, but his hair was gray and cropped close to his head. The awkward quality that had put me at ease was gone. I sat down in a chair and scanned his office for something familiar. I fastened on the fabric-covered couch, on which I had so many times bared my soul.

It was odd to be looking at him as he looked at me. I noted the deep lines etched between his eyebrows and around his mouth, like gashes in wood. His face had a certain cruelty in repose, I thought, but twenty years had elapsed since we had last met. Sun and the passage of time, I told myself, had hardened his face. Though he was a child psychiatrist, I saw no trace of children's toys, crayons, or blocks. Some part of me, I realized, had hoped I would be able to play instead of talk.

Twenty years was a long time not to have seen my analyst, and we did not pick up where we had left off as easily as I had with Robbie. Dr. M. looked so hardened to me that I imagined a string of career reversals, disappointments, divorce, lawsuits. His assistant had said he practiced psychopharmacology: I wondered if he abused the drugs he prescribed.

Dr. M.'s body filled his Eames chair and his long legs stretched out like a spider's. As I sat facing him, his head dissolved before my eyes and morphed into the face of a dissipated Roman emperor, then the face of Humpty Dumpty, then of Jiminy Cricket. Was I going crazy?

Nothing like this had ever happened to me before, certainly not as an adult. It was important for me to hide it from Dr. M. I tried to ignore his morphing face and say what came to mind despite it. Only later did I allow myself to write down my associations: Humpty Dumpty sat on the wall, Humpty Dumpty had a great fall. Jiminy Cricket was Pinocchio's conscience; Pinocchio lied and was kidnapped by a puppeteer; my nanny Milena's hobby was puppetry. I played with her puppets.

I worked so hard to seem normal during that first in-person session that I didn't at first hear Dr. M. say, "We have to stop." Then I stood up, put on my coat, and hurried off to see friends downtown.

I created an entertaining story for them and, as I described his face morphing, I realized that his office had morphed too. When I walked in, my eyes had registered a Persian carpet, pleasant wooden furniture and bookshelves. Now, I recalled gray metal shelves; an ugly metal desk; metal chairs, like an office of the 1950s.

My friends, preparing for a class they were about to teach, pooh-poohed my fantasy of a corrupt Dr. M. and I was happy to laugh it off as some kind of aberration. But during the four hours it took to return home, I mulled over those unusual things my mind was doing. Maybe I should have looked for a local therapist. Stick with the enemy you know, I thought, and only later realized that I had adapted one of the idioms my father learned in night school: better the devil you know than the devil you don't know.

~ 22 ~

Of the many ways people refuse to admit what they know, I employed some of the most basic. Instead of identifying the problem as my engineer husband would, I doubted, minimized, or ignored what was too painful to acknowledge. I had quit therapy — twice — to avoid remembering childhood molestation. It would have made sense, once I'd chosen to return to Dr. M., to trust his competence, but I kept second-guessing it.

Not only did many 21st century therapists find psychoanalysis obsolete, but I had accepted Dr. Young's referral of Dr. M. years before without question or investigation. In fact, I knew almost nothing about him and refrained from finding out.

After casting him as a corrupt Roman, I imagined him as a lepidopterist with a butterfly net. He flushed out my fluttering associations and, one by one, pinned them to a board for classification. I didn't have to search far for the meaning of this association: tall, formal Vladimir Nabokov was the only lepidopterist I knew of. He was my mother's favorite author and his novel *Lolita* was widely discussed in the refugee community when I was a child. Its protagonist, Humbert Humbert, was a pedophile.

Somehow, that detailed association didn't translate for me into the fact that I distrusted my analyst. Though Dr. M. had so far responded effectively to my distress, I found myself challenging his expertise. How could he grasp the complicated cultural context of my childhood? And how could he be unaffected by the patriarchal theories in which he had been trained? What boy had ever identified with Tiger Lily instead of Peter Pan? Or with any of the Little Women? Or with Helen Keller? When Helen finally managed to understand language and produced the word "Water," it sounded like a howl.

I couldn't make any sound. I was speechless with disbelief, and what I only later understood as fear and shame. But as I disparaged Dr. M., I kept in mind the reasons I had chosen to work with him again. He was an expert on many things important to me: childhood, parenting, adolescence, the interpretation of dreams. Yet I even restricted what I told him about my dreams.

I kept dreaming of eggplants, leeks, cucumbers and squash served on the elegant china my mother used for parties and customers. It was obvious that these were phallic vegetables. I didn't want to discuss the meaning of their being eaten with Dr. M. After all, he was a man, with a sexual appetite, trained in a phallo-centric school of psychology.

But sometimes my wish to be a good patient won out over my strategies of denial. I managed to tell Dr. M. a dream about a disembodied penis — whose? — lying on a table glossy with shellac. It referred, I thought, to Ivan's hair and lamps, but also to a painting I had made, at age 22, when I was staying with an artist friend at her family's cottage. Robbie — who was living nearby — visited, and we had slept together in her childhood room. After he left, I borrowed her oil paints and a brush and painted a small, gleaming canvas.

Dr. M. refrained from much interpretation in those first few months. I was grateful not to have to deal with his stuff in addition to mine. But even though I felt I was in good hands I kept questioning my analyst's competence, demanding to know how much of his training was antiquated Freud. He said, "I've been trained in lots of ways" until I gave up on that.

I didn't at first describe how I shouted into the water as I swam every day, or the choking sensation in my throat that sometimes became so strong and disturbing that I would have to stop driving and sit at the wheel taking deep breaths to calm down. I felt like I was choking on frogs and I thought Dr. M. would think I was manufacturing symptoms. Was I?

I began systematically reading through the history of treatment of childhood sexual assault. That history had been written mostly by male psychiatrists starting with Freud. At first, Freud had regarded the accounts of molestation he heard from female patients as memories. Then he changed his mind and regarded them as fantasies.

I read his case study of the young patient he dubbed "Dora" and thought he had treated her like a lock to be picked rather than a patient to be healed. A bit like Professor Henry Higgins and his project Eliza Doolittle. Same period. Neither professor seemed capable of seeing the world through his charge's eyes. Good therapy, I thought, required a level playing field, not a hierarchy. I wondered if Dr. M. modeled himself on Freud. If so, how could I trust my care to him?

After undermining my faith in my doctor, I praised him. I owed my marriage and family to Dr. M. He was smart, principled, funny, and worked with troubled children. I wish someone had sent me to a child psychiatrist back then! After defending him, I reminded myself not to. I had grown up defending the adults and where had that led?

Language itself was another battlefield on which I fought on both sides. When Dr. M. talked about my "suffering," I rejected rather than accepted the word. It struck me as a euphemism, an inadequate verbal bandage for a deep and knotty wound. Maybe no word was adequate. No word could adequately describe the experience of sexual assault, convey its overwhelming confusion of real and unreal. That problem of finding a language, I thought, was compounded by cultural appropriation. Once fresh and helpful terms like "breaking silence," "building self-esteem," and "sharing stories" all became stale. The alchemy of repetition transformed them into cliché and then material for satire.

Then there was the issue of a hierarchy of suffering. My molestation had been relatively minor in the larger scheme of things. I hadn't been gang-raped or forced by a family member to have regular sex like many abused girls I read about. Childhood sexual abuse was nothing compared to the war. It wasn't "suffering" as I understood the word.

I had been taught — consciously or unconsciously — a concrete hierarchy of suffering. As the daughter of Holocaust survivors and refugees from Communism, I had been a fortunate child, living out the American dream. I could not and did not wish to view myself as a victim.

Victims were the pitiful women on a popular television show called Queen for a Day who competed by telling the viewers tragic stories of their lives and what they needed to fix them. A studio audience applause meter determined whose misfortune was the most compelling. She was crowned, draped in a fur-trimmed cape, then rewarded with a washing machine, a refrigerator, sometimes a vacation. Once, a former concentration camp inmate told about her experience and said that she relived it every time she looked at the tattoo on her forearm. She was awarded what was then a rare and costly skin graft as prize.

In 2001, a combination of feminism and political correctness had made the designation of "victim" even more unattractive, its connotations of passivity and powerlessness degrading to 21st century American women.

The term "survivor" had replaced it: cancer survivor, rape survivor, transforming the word that had once meant "escaping death at the meanest level" into a synonym for heroine. "Veteran" was a better word, I thought. I wanted a better word for "sexual abuse," too. But no name could satisfy me. None was broad enough or signified enough outrage.

Or maybe my fury about language was a substitute for fury at Ivan and my parents and yet another way to avoid addressing it.

I told Robbie much of what I didn't tell Dr. M.: how I wanted to dive into memory and, at the next moment, not touch it with a ten-foot pole. How I fell into altered states of consciousness without warning. How a sound or smell could set me sobbing or hyperventilating. How I imagined frogs in my throat; even delivering a baby out of my throat.

I was afraid Dr. M. would interpret that as a consequence of my brother being born when I was three. He was big on the impact of younger siblings and had several times floated the idea of my jealousy of a baby brother displacing me as the focus of my parents' love.

My constant criticism aside, it was, however, ever more obvious to me how dependent I was becoming on my analyst. I counted on hearing his voice on the answering machine. The message was like a ritual blessing. I was rattled if he picked up the phone and interrupted the recording and even more rattled if the line was busy. I'd redial three, four, five times, in snowballing alarm. "Is everything OK?" I'd ask. Or, "Are you running late?"

I didn't express the panic I felt when I couldn't reach him or say, "I was afraid you were dead."

~ 23 ~

I took pride in hiding all this from my family. I wasn't going to burden my children and spouse with the residue of events that had taken place before they came on the scene the way my own mother had done. I was organizing my younger son's *bar mitzvah,* a modest event but one requiring co-ordination with the tutor, the rabbi, the printer, and caterer; negotiating with family members about accommodations and participation. And then, a year after I had visited him in California, Robbie called while I was making dinner. Would I meet him in New York?

"When," I asked, hoping he wouldn't say "Tomorrow."

"Next month."

I tried to tamp down my excitement and focus on the *bar mitzvah.* Though I am not an observant Jew, I saw the event as the culmination of what Judaism defines as childhood, and was relieved that both my sons had now reached it safely.

Jewish tradition requires children to study a portion of Torah, grapple with the meaning of their text, then speak about it to their community. My son faced his audience calm and well prepared. He chanted his portion in Hebrew in a deep voice, then explained in English what he had understood. Looking up at him as he towered over the Rabbi, I thought — not for the first time — how different his upbringing had been from my own.

He had grown up with a group of parental figures, including his daycare teachers. I had learned a lot about my son as well as about parenting him from them. When, instead of napping, he tried to charm his teachers into long chats, they went along with him. They gave him feedback when he did something well, and if I didn't provide it in sufficient measure, he learned to provide it himself. "Good job," he would congratulate himself as a little boy. "Good job."

While Patrick found this American overkill, I vacillated between envy and delight. As a child, I had rarely been praised and, often, told not to let success go to my head. From the moment they emerged from my body and Patrick cut their umbilical cords, I had been aware of the separateness of my sons. Unlike my mother's sense of being just like me, my awareness of their difference never disappeared.

But I also remembered how uneasy I had been about leaving them with babysitters. I was afraid, I thought in retrospect, to leave them with an unsupervised adult.

Apart from their relaxed disciplinary style, I thought, the teachers at daycare taught me a different model of dealing with upset than the one familiar to me. One day my son came home repeating, "Big noise, Mama, big noise," with a note explaining that a fire alarm had gone off at daycare that afternoon and that it had blared for several minutes. The children would need help from their parents to "process" it.

"Big noise," he repeated for several days.

"Yes, big noise," I repeated back to him, as per the suggestion. "It was a fire drill."

After a week, he would say, "Let's talk about the fire." This continued for several more weeks and though it got old, I had taken pleasure in repeating our dialogue again and again until he put the experience to rest.

At the *bar mitzvah,* the rabbi blessed all of us who had helped our son grow up. I caught myself admiring my tall husband, the crow's feet around his eyes, the dimples in his cheeks when he smiled. Like our sons, Patrick seemed to have gotten through childhood untraumatized. He rarely questioned his ability to meet a challenge, and attributed my insecurities to an artistic rather than scientific bent. He regarded me as his *moitié,* or complementary half and never questioned the stability of our marriage. Once again, I thought he was like my father in this regard. Patrick was unworried about my ongoing collaboration with Robbie or my meeting him in New York.

I was a little worried. It would be the first time I saw him in person since my revelation about Ivan. Visiting our old haunts in Manhattan would surely be different from seeing him in California. The last time Robbie and I had seen each other in the city, just before I decided to get married, we had wound up in my bed. I felt both giddy and unprotected.

Two days before Robbie and I were to meet, he still hadn't decided where to stay. That vagueness was familiar to me but difficult to square with my family calendar. I didn't know how to plan, whether I'd spend one or two days in the city, see Dr. M. or drive back with Robbie to Massachusetts. Finally he called and suggested a time and place to meet. Girlfriends who knew what I was doing advised me to call home often and make sure to look into mirrors — anything to resist the undertow of the past. I was pleased by their concern, but knew that warnings were useless. When Robbie appeared at our meeting place, we hugged. Unlike the last time we met, in California, I wasn't numb; I felt a strong flush of pleasure in my body.

"Don't you miss the city?" Robbie asked as he opened the door of his rented car.

I did miss the city, I thought as I sat down in my long cherished place beside him. I missed museums, theaters, concert halls and many of the friends I'd left behind. I missed knowing where everything was and how to get there. But I had also felt a strong need to leave and I didn't want to come back.

We drove through our old neighborhoods, through the now gentrified Hell's Kitchen of his childhood and the Upper West Side of mine, north up the West Side Highway. The roads were empty, most people at work more conventional than ours. Robbie finally wanted to show me what he never had wanted me to see when we were teenagers.

~ 24 ~

Robbie stopped at the deserted beachfront of the left-wing colony where his father and stepmother rented a bungalow every summer. He pointed out the pavilion where he led his chorus of children in spirituals and Schubert, the rocks where he had gone fishing with his father, the spots where he had necked with his girlfriends.

I suggested we walk around the lake and Robbie reminded me that he couldn't walk. Instead, he drove down the main street of the town on the river where he had been a teenager: past the high school, library, and post office. On one side were the "flats" where he had lived, near the railroad tracks and the auto plant where his stepfather was a union organizer. He showed me the union hall where he had first performed music. Then he drove up the hill to the fancy side of town, to the house where his friend Mike, the doctor's son, still lived. His mother had never been invited there, Robbie said. His father was — but only once.

We could stay at Mike's overnight, Robbie said, as though the thought had just occurred to him — which perhaps it had. We could drive back into the city, go to the concert, and drive back. In the morning, we'd have a head start to Massachusetts.

I was delighted to hear he would drive me home.

It was six by the time we sat down in a restaurant near Lincoln Center. I had grown up around the corner in the 1950s, babysat down the street for two young families. I read their books, raided their refrigerators, listened to their records, and wondered about their marriages. One couple — the one I thought beautiful and artistic — told me they were separating a few months after their second child was born.

"I visited when you babysat on Riverside Drive," Robbie said. "There was a baby grand. We sat on the floor, listening to records."

"Weren't you going out on dates?"

"I didn't have money," he said. "When your mother got us tickets to the Czech Philharmonic it was a huge deal for me."

Dinner with Robbie was a huge deal for me. We had never dined in a restaurant together. The waiter gave us menus and, citing the French, Robbie asked me to order. I did, wondering what marriage to him would have been like.

Like our roller-coaster ride at Coney Island, I thought. Breathtaking highs, plummeting lows, and stomach-churning anxiety in between. Like being married to my mother. With both of them, I lost track of who was who.

The street was dark by the time Robbie paid. A river of traffic flowed through the crowded Lincoln Center intersection, as we stood surrounded by well-dressed concertgoers. The white buildings were brightly lit; the fountain sent a sparkling jet of water into the air.

"May I take your arm?" I surprised myself by asking. Robbie smiled and crooked his elbow. Then halfway across, he grabbed my hand and for a long, uncomfortable minute, I held his. When we reached the other side, I dropped it. I didn't want to be seen holding hands.

We sat in the orchestra, not the balcony where I had sat for so many years with my mother. Smoking was no longer permitted in the corridors and the refugee audience was long dead, but I felt as though they were there around me. Brahms' Third Symphony opened the program. Robbie had played a recording in his basement room the first time we made love and I teared up with the opening bars.

I was relieved that my glasses and the dim light served as concealers. Maybe Robbie's eyesight was really bad or I was extraordinarily adept at dissimulation. At any rate, he didn't notice my distress and, during intermission, launched into a critique of the conductor.

He was still dissecting the performance when close to midnight, we pulled into the driveway of a house on the top of the hill overlooking the river. I had been to a party inside that house 37 years earlier. Mike let us in. He and Robbie had cemented a bond in Mississippi: show up anytime, with anyone, no questions asked. It reminded me of my parents' bond with other survivors: unequivocal.

The house looked exactly as I remembered it from decades before: like a set for a play about America in 1965.

We talked in the kitchen until two in the morning when Mike's wife gave us towels and led us to the children's wing: two small bedrooms across the hall from one another, crammed with left-behind kid stuff.

In the bathroom, I washed up and remembered a friend's advice to look into the mirror, recognize the present, and resist the undertow of the past. I saw not a teenage girl, but a happy, excited middle-aged woman, regretful, confused, sad, nostalgic, alert.

I went into my room and called out "Your turn."

Through the thin walls, I heard Robbie perform his ablutions. We had spent sixteen hours together by then and, lying in a teenager's bed, looking up at her posters, I was, for what seemed like the first time, conscious of the sexual attraction I had not felt when I was myself a teenager.

Back then, Robbie had affected me the way Kryptonite affected Superman: I became weak and passive in his presence, lost my bounce and agency. Now I began to suspect that I had put a lid on feeling.

Robbie called out good night, closed the door to his bedroom, and I soon heard a loud, droning snore.

I tossed and turned in my narrow bed, trying to make sense of a confusion of half-grasped ideas. I had decided to reconnect with the idea of revisiting a troubling adolescent love. In working with him, I had retrieved a memory of molestation and my mother's long affair with my molester. I had chosen Robbie to navigate this terrain with me because he knew the players, was fascinated by all varieties of experience, and because I needed a witness.

Our respective spouses made my project possible, and I was acutely conscious of not betraying their trust. That was what my mother had done with Ivan, indulged a sexual passion so strong that it lasted for years and blinded her to everything else. She had taken it for granted that I resembled her in this way as in so many others.

Until her death, she thought of me as her double — intellectually, physically and psychologically. When she met Patrick's parents before we were married, Franci told me later, conversation had turned to the unconventional matter of my being six years older than their son. Patrick's mother had said that my age might lead her son astray some day. Franci had confidently assured her that, if anyone were to be unfaithful, it would be me. My mother had related this conversation to me soon after it took place.

How much of my relationship with Robbie had to do with her life and how much with my own? I wondered as I tossed on that teenager's bed. I was glad that Robbie had, sometime earlier in the day, made clear the boundaries of our current relationship. We were both married now, he said. Our marriages were unlike those of our parents.

I was, as my mother had foreseen, less sure. I felt dizzy and confused, as if I had been riding an elevator up and down my psyche, stopping at five, fifteen and fifty — as though those ages were floors in an apartment building. At each stop, I wondered: when does intimacy become infidelity? Why is verbal intercourse permissible and sexual intercourse proscribed? What constitutes transgression?

~ 25 ~

I woke up to the sounds of Robbie showering. Together, we prepared breakfast in the unfamiliar kitchen, ate in silence, washed the dishes and hit the road.

I had felt safe being his passenger ever since he used to drive me home from chorus, even when Robbie drove a motorcycle. We both enjoyed riding through late-night Manhattan, my breasts against his back, my arms holding onto him. One night we were midway down a long hill in the rain when a tire blew. I held my breath, he balanced on the slippery asphalt and we glided to a stop.

With that in mind, I screwed up my courage and broached the question that had been on my mind for months: did he remember the first time we slept together?

Robbie gave me an inquiring glance. "Yes. Why?"

I had never understood what had happened that night. It had been traumatic and confusing and was still bothering me. He had witnessed what happened. It would help me to know what he had seen and understood.

"Okay."

"I had to talk you into having sex, right?"

"No. Why would you have had to talk me into it?"

"I remember arguing about it outside my parents' house."

He kept his eyes on the road. "Maybe I didn't want to risk messing things up. You were stability for me. I depended upon your approval."

I forced myself to continue. "I remember driving to your mother's house, getting out and walking in the dark."

"That's right," he said. "My room was in the basement."

"You shut the door and I remember just standing there."

My throat closed. Then I forced myself to speak again. "Do you think you could have taken your penis out and said, 'This is my penis.'?"

"No," Robbie said. "Definitely not."

Tears began sliding out of my eyes again. I had been so sure of that part. But the fact was that by the age of 20, I had seen others, men I knew and men I did not, unzip their pants.

He drove for a few more miles before he said, "I think you're mixing me up with someone. What else do you remember?"

I remembered his bed, the music of Brahms, then rocketing out of my body and looking down from the ceiling. I wanted Robbie to make sense of it all for me: confirm that it happened; explain how and why I had left my body, and why I had held onto the memory of it for so long. But something kept me from speaking.

Robbie couldn't answer what I didn't ask.

"It's unrealistic to expect you to remember what actually happened," I said.

"No it's not," Robbie replied. "It was an unusual sexual experience. You seemed transfixed, like you stopped breathing."

I wanted him to elaborate but Robbie moved on. "What happened the next day was stranger. We went on a drive and your mother came with us. She sat in the front seat. You sat in the back."

"I probably invited her," I said. "I shared everything with her back then."

"But you gave up your place to her. It was surreal."

Really? I didn't question my behavior. "She always sat in the front. A roof collapsed on her back in the war."

"So what?" said Robbie, "It was our date."

Our date, not my mother's. Why was that so hard for me to understand? I had a recording of Franci lecturing to a college class about surviving the war, telling the roof story. A perceptive student asks how she felt when her daughter was the age my mother had been in the camps. Franci replies, "Of course I was jealous." I had heaved a sigh of relief. "I always sensed it but I never had proof."

"I felt she was jealous of you," Robbie said.

Maybe that's why the note in my journal about my night with Robbie was written in Hebrew, a language my mother didn't know. I rarely wrote anything in Hebrew.

"I certainly felt it with my first serious boyfriend. She seemed to want me to marry him more than I did."

"Literary Man?"

"No," I said. "She hated him."

Tall, blond, from Kansas, he reminded my mother, she remarked more than once, of Nazi youth, and lost few opportunities to make disparaging remarks. When we moved into my lake cottage for the summer to write, Franci looked around the premises, lit a cigarette and said, "What do you plan to do here all summer — bake pies?"

She had brought as a housewarming present four aluminum folding chairs, beach chairs of the 1950s. When she had floated the idea, I had told her I didn't like them. Now, I asked her to return them. Franci had — for the only time I remember — called me a bitch and raised her hand to slap me. Then my boyfriend was between us, saying if she hit me, he'd hit her back. She left.

It was the first time I defended my territory from my mother. I was deeply shaken.

"It wasn't until after she died that I understood I was scared of her," I told Robbie. "Did you know it?"

"You were the girl who hitch-hiked through Europe alone. I didn't think you were scared of anyone."

I had hitch-hiked alone, thinking I was protected by my height, my American passport, the cigarettes I kept lighting and holding in my left hand. My brain refused to acknowledge danger. When I recounted my escapades to Dr. M. during our first round of analysis, he had interpreted my hitch-hiking as risk-taking, counter-phobic behavior. I thought he had led a coddled, sheltered life and dismissed his interpretation back then. But he had been right: my default reaction to danger was to deny it.

I told Robbie about another bizarre episode where I had not risen up out of my body, just lost all connection to it. Two strange men broke into the apartment where he had visited me in the 1970s. My roommate was typing. Then her typing stopped; she called my name. I looked up from my bed where I was reading and saw a tall man standing in the hallway between our rooms. In a spectacular feat of dissociation, I pretended he wasn't there and continued reading.

What followed is encoded in my brain like a dance, with myself as choreographer. My roommate calls my name again. She's standing in the hallway now, in a long flannel nightgown and her granny glasses, dwarfed by the intruder.

I get off my bed, stride over and ask, "What do you want?"

"Hey, I'm a junkie. I need your money..." he replies in a slow, sluggish drone. Then a shorter man appears from our living room. He is gesturing with a knife. My eyes take in my roommate trembling and the two men, and I remember the hold-ups on TV shows of my childhood.

The trouble is we own almost nothing. I tell the robbers I'll give them our money, collect a total of $50 from our wallets and hand it over to the guy with the knife.

He takes it, and then opens the door to our linen closet and points. My roommate tries to fold herself into it.

"Hey man," I say, saying lines I must have adapted from some movie. "We're so scared, we won't call the cops. We'll go into the bathroom and stay there until you leave."

The short man motions us into the bathroom and tries to close the door. It has a metal stopper at its base that jams. We push; he pulls. I give up and, holding my roommate's hand, lead her into the bathtub with me, our faces away from the men, away from the door, willing them to leave. When we hear our front door close, we embrace and call the police.

"You were lucky," was all Robbie said.

I had dined out for years on my mugging story, making a joke of it, garnering laughs; Robbie's response made me examine it again. What mechanism in my psyche had enabled me to first ignore the man standing in my hallway, then take charge of their robbery? Why had I suggested that my roommate and I stand in the bathtub facing the wall? Were they linked to the story in the photo albums I wanted to examine together with Robbie?

~ 26 ~

We pulled into my driveway just before six. My new house, with its two-car garage, looked embarrassingly large. Inside was my family, ready for dinner. I felt like a moon pulled between the magnetic fields of two opposing planets.

Encircled by my husband, two hungry boys, and an excited dog, I snapped into my role of Marine sergeant: directing one son to take Robbie's suitcase to the basement; the other to set the table; catching up on domestic news, assembling the ingredients of a makeshift dinner.

Patrick welcomed our guest — he had met Robbie years before and liked him — but he was too preoccupied with Town Meeting that night to engage him in conversation. There was no cognac, no home-cooked *goulash* with dumplings, nothing resembling dinner with my family in Manhattan. My three guys were friendly but not particularly curious, accustomed to adult friends at dinner. Robbie looked shell-shocked.

After a quick, unceremonious meal, my sons cleaned their plates, put their plates in the dishwasher and disappeared. Patrick left for Town Meeting. I was so flustered by the collision of my past and present, that I was surprised when Robbie reminded me of the photo album I had told him about.

"Aren't you tired?" I asked.

"Yes," he said quietly, "but I want to see it."

I was tired too but grateful to Robbie. He went down to the basement; I retrieved the small, well-worn, book-sized binder.

After my mother died, I had emptied her apartment and discovered it on a bookshelf in her bedroom. I didn't remember ever seeing it though it was clearly marked FRANCI-FRANOVÉ on its spine.

Ivan had executed the red crayon lettering in 1955. I had been seven years old then and accustomed to Ivan taking photographs and pasting them in albums. The ones he made for me featured scenes of birthday parties and picnics in the woods, interspersed with newspaper and magazine cut-outs, captions indicating where and when.

My mother's album was similar in style but very different in content: it was a document of erotic obsession, and I had reacted to it in a similar way to the appearance of strange men in my apartment. I refused to integrate it into my consciousness. Now, I carried it downstairs, wanting Robbie to help me.

He was lying on his back on the guest bed like a beached whale. I settled cross-legged on the bed beside him and, when he didn't sit up, opened the album on his chest.

"The cover page says *Crazy Success of Franové* in French," I translated for Robbie as much as for myself. "FRANOVÉ was the name of her *salon* then. Notice the octopus on the left."

He looked at a small illustration of eight blue arms holding cups of jello and said, "Tell me the story again."

I was glad he asked: no matter how many times I thought or wrote it, the story of my mother and my nanny's husband sounded incredible to me.

Ivan and his wife Milena were refugees, 20 years older than my mother. Both came from prominent Czech families. My mother often said, with deference, that their paths would never have crossed in Prague.

Ivan had been the editor of a large anti-Nazi newspaper before the war. When the Germans invaded, he was among the first arrested. Though not a Jew, he had been interned in concentration camp for six years — twice as long as my parents. While he was in camp, Milena had been in Prague with their son, and had risked their lives by hiding a little girl who was Jewish.

When the war ended in 1945, Ivan returned to work at his newspaper and was known as a vocal anti-Communist. The mother of the little girl Milena had hidden *was* a Communist. She reclaimed her daughter and refused to let her even visit the woman who had saved her life. After the Communists seized power, Ivan, Milena and their son fled the country.

They arrived in New York, 50 years old, with no money and no English. Milena heard through the refugee grapevine that my mother was looking for a nanny.

"All of us fell in love," my mother used to say and, explaining it as a woman of 50 myself, I could see how the pieces had fit: Milena was mourning the little girl she had lost; my mother was mourning her murdered parents; Ivan was a hero and fellow camp survivor; my father and Milena hit it off; they all spoke the same language.

I turned to the second page.

Red lipstick was her trademark, I told Robbie. I remembered her opening her silver lipstick holder at concerts. She rarely left home without it.

"What did Kurt think of Ivan?" Robbie asked.

I didn't know, I said, but I could guess. Ivan was a drinker, smoker, loudmouth — not a sportsman or gentleman. But bottom line: they had all been on the same side — during the war and after it.

"Tell me what's going on here," Robbie said.

Silver Point beach, I explained, was the refugee version of his parents' left-wing summer colony. Ivan had taken a photo of my parents lying together on the sand, then pasted it into a drawing of an old-fashioned girdle. The typed caption, as I translated it from the Czech, read *"a corset that doesn't pinch."*

Šněrovačka, která netlačí.

"How old is everyone?"

"My mother was 35; my father 51; Ivan and Milena, 55. I was seven. My brother had turned four that spring."

My mother said I had been three when I told her she and Ivan looked married.

When had I started complaining about Ivan chasing me into corners to kiss me?

Robbie kept quiet, examining the photographs like the man in the movie *Blow-Up* who searched photograph after photograph for clues to a crime. He remained on his back, perfectly still. Maybe he had done this before, with another old girlfriend. If the statistics were correct, at least two or three of us would have been molested as children.

He pointed to another photo of my parents lying in the sand, my mother's head on my father's thigh.

"Translation?"

"At the foot of her slave."

Then came a photograph I had seen before — in my own album: my three-year-old brother, naked, urinating on the sand like the Belgian statue while my father looked on. In my mother's album, Ivan had drawn a red arrow pointing to my brother's penis. His text read: *"Look, Franci, what you don't have! S. Freud."*

Robbie said nothing but I was pretty sure that in his family, children weren't photographed urinating. I tended to dismiss Dr. M.'s view that the casual nudity of my parents had been over-stimulating to me as a child, but looking at this page with Robbie, I saw my analyst's point.

We looked at an illustration of elegant legs and I translated the caption for him: *"Almost like Franci."*

Another page of red lips and white teeth captioned *"Before pleasure and after; with teeth and without."* Then, under a photo of my mother, my brother and me sitting on my father's back, a caption seemingly addressed to my father: *"According to Lincoln: that's no burden — it's my family."* And under a bouquet of red roses, *"Take care that your most beautiful flower doesn't wilt."*

Kurte, pozor! Aby Vám ta nej-
hezčí neuvadla!

Even with Robbie witnessing my show-translate-and-tell, I was unable to translate what I was seeing into what it meant.

Robbie didn't ask me what I was thinking or feeling. He kept silent as I continued to translate, just pointed to parts of snapshots and parts of illustrations that particularly struck him. His silence had been wise as well as kind, I thought in retrospect. Robbie was certainly familiar with marital infidelity but I suspected that even he found the album unnerving.

Finally we reached the end. Inside the back cover, Ivan had glued a headshot of himself.

He had typed the only English caption: *"The Author."*

We closed the album. Robbie said we would talk in the morning. I went upstairs, undressed and folded myself into the warmth of my sleeping husband.

~ 27 ~

The next morning, Robbie waited for all three of my guys to leave the house before he came upstairs, refused breakfast and said he'd pick up coffee at Starbucks. I didn't argue. I remembered my own complicated reactions to dinner in his home out west. Instead I suggested we drive to Starbucks before I showed him Lexington and Concord.

"Does there have to be a plan?" he asked acidly.

"When you have kids, yes," I said, remembering that he had none. He had offered to go piano shopping with my younger son after he got out of school. "He's out at three. We have six hours. But we can cancel if you like."

Robbie shook his head. He drove to Starbucks and, as he got his coffee, I sat in his rented car and tried to recollect how shocked I, myself, had been by moving to this town just two years before. I no longer found its pristine beauty strange; I enjoyed and admired it. But Robbie seemed to be having a strong reaction to my new surroundings. He expressed no interest in the historic landmarks that busloads of tourists from all over the world come to see. I insisted that we drive along the revolutionary road, past the picturesque stone walls and battlefields of the American Revolution, but seeing that he barely gave them a glance, I cut short the tour and directed him to the highway.

I had planned lunch with artist friends in Cape Ann whom I thought he'd like. I loved to sit in their loft crammed with paintings and electronics, look out at the harbor and listen to the cries of seagulls. I imagined that we would discuss art and creative process like four characters in a D.H. Lawrence novel.

Robbie turned on the radio when we got on the highway. Then five minutes from our destination, he pulled off at a Friendly's, saying, "I need protein."

I had vowed not to re-enter another Friendly's once my children were grown, but I didn't argue. I just phoned my friend Lisa that we'd be late. Then I sat in the familiar booth as Robbie ate a tuna fish sandwich and I reflected on some of our many differences.

It was only when I was ringing Lisa's doorbell that I remembered there was no elevator. There were two flights of stairs to her loft and I led the way slowly, Robbie breathing heavily behind me.

Once he had sat down for a few minutes, Robbie became his sociable, attractive self. He looked carefully at Lisa's paintings but seemed at a loss for words, with less to say than my engineer husband. I remembered that art museums had not been part of Robbie's Communist childhood. Why had I expected him to be able to discuss contemporary art?

He regained his authority over lunch. He and Max were both of the Vietnam generation, ex-New Yorkers and dropouts both. They spoke the same language and their conversation moved from music, to computers, to meds. Lisa and I exchanged glances as we listened to them talk.

I was interested but kept one eye on the clock. Just before two, I broke in to say we had to leave, that Robbie was helping us buy a piano. The good-byes were cordial and, going down the stairs, Robbie told me how much he had enjoyed my friends.

I thought he would, I said, as we got into the car. He and Max were as like as two peas in a pod. Same intensity, same working-class style. Watching them, I said, I had understood how the civil rights movement had spawned women's liberation: the men talked while the women served coffee.

I didn't realize how provocative that remark sounded. At first he said nothing. Then, he exploded.

What was I talking about? Hadn't he looked long enough at my friend's paintings? Asked questions? He, Robbie, hadn't asked Lisa to wait on him. I was the one who waited on men who didn't respect me for it.

"Don't project your fucking life onto me!" he muttered as he accelerated down the interstate. I was a writer. A creative woman. Instead of organizing my life around my family, I should hire an au pair!

"An au pair?" I repeated, amused to hear him use the term. "If I hired a housekeeper, you'd say I was exploiting her."

Robbie disregarded that and continued to argue the indignity of my serving my sons and husband. It was a line of argument that I was accustomed to making to my spouse and it was both funny and disconcerting to hear it from Robbie.

"All of what you're saying is true," I replied. "But I wanted to have children and I wanted to be a different kind of mother than my mother. You're right that it's hard to get enough time to work, but I manage. And you'll notice that I've managed to spend three whole days with you."

It occurred to me that he might be confusing me with his mother. But, unlike Tess, I wasn't poor or mentally ill. I had two very healthy children and a husband who made enough money so when I didn't feel like cooking or wanted a vacation, I didn't have to think twice about either.

But Robbie just amped up the volume. "You've got to stop pretending! You are very very unhappy! And pretending that you're happy and that things are OK is not healthy."

Unhappy? Pretending? "Could you try not to yell?"

"Could you stop being so afraid of anger?"

I braced my feet against the floor — against collision as well as Robbie's continuing eruption. I felt frightened but acutely aware of the feeling; I was pleased to be staying present in my body and even able to respond in words.

“I’m not unhappy,” I said, when he took a breath. “Maybe I’m not living in the way you imagined I should live, but I like my life. I like my husband and my kids. I’m even beginning to like living in the suburbs.”

I didn’t add that, after thinking long and hard, I had decided that living with another artist was not a good option for me. I’d tried it and remembered the entangling highs and lows, the often insidious, sometimes explicit vying for time and attention, trying to maintain a balance between needs. I had chosen a partner whose professional life held little interest for me, but whom I found interesting in his own right. He loved me whether or not I wrote well, liked to walk through life with me. Three days with Robbie confirmed the wisdom of my choice.

“You’re like some fucking timekeeper,” he was railing on. “Ten o’clock here. Two o’clock there. You’re so afraid of standing still and actually feeling anything that you don’t allow life to happen.”

“I’m sorry,” I said.

“I’m not some pawn to be moved from place to place!”

“No you’re not.”

As he continued ranting and barreling down the highway, I began to cry. I wondered if we should forget about looking for a piano. I tried to breathe deeply and tune Robbie out. When he came to the end of one complaint, he started from the top again. Maybe he had had as impossible expectations of me as I had had of him and was deeply disappointed in who I had become.

“I told you I didn’t want to see battlefields.”

“I said I was sorry about the battlefields,” I apologized again. “You like to drive. You like history. It took 10 minutes.”

“Well, suppose I don’t want to see anything? Isn’t that my right? Don’t I have a choice?”

Before I had a chance to reply, Robbie was off again. But enough was enough.

“Look,” I interrupted, “this is the third time I’m apologizing. It’s the last. You’re not going to yell at me in front of my son. I’m not going to cry in front of him.”

Robbie pulled into a gas station and got out of the car to refuel. I went to the restroom. My eyes were puffy, my mouth swollen. My mother would have pulled out her little silver case and reapplied her lipstick, but I never wore lipstick and just splashed water on my face. By the time I got back, Robbie was back behind the wheel. "Do you still want to shop for a piano?" I asked.

"Why not?" he replied. While I was in the washroom his mood had shifted. "Wasn't that the plan?"

"It was," I said, then directed him to follow the line of cars turning into the middle school parking lot.

My son spotted me waving and clambered into the back seat. He was, as Robbie had been at 13, already a musician. He had been playing on a hand-me-down upright for several years. Now for mysterious reasons linked to Robbie, he was getting a new one.

I had been just a year older than my son when I met Robbie, probably as fresh, energetic, but not as self-absorbed. I had been more attuned to my mother than to myself. As we drove away from school, I was still feeling shaken but I asked him my usual questions about his day.

Robbie drove in silence to an industrial park where an entire floor of a former mill had been converted into a showroom. Inside, on a bare expanse of wooden planks, framed by bare brick walls, were hundreds of gleaming pianos — spinets, uprights, concert grands, baby grands, Steinways, Baldwins, Yamahas. Flags of many countries hung from pipes in the ceiling, giving the scene the quality of a medieval pageant. We were the only customers and, after a moment in which we stood still, taking it in, Robbie and my musician son, each following his own inclination, began playing piano after piano.

Watching the two of them move from keyboard to keyboard was like watching children in a playground. My son tried out bits of a summer camp anthem and a Mozart sonata he was learning; my first love, bits of Joni Mitchell and Beatles, then a Chopin nocturne. I sat down on a piano stool opposite the baby grand where Robbie had settled. As he looked up from the keyboard, his eyes lit up at me in the way I remembered. Then he bent over the keyboard and jauntily played the first few bars of the piece I had first heard him perform in Mr. Labovitz's studio so many years before.

His fingers were no longer supple but his playing still sounded as though he was telling a story. Even though I felt bruised by his anger, I understood how essential he had been to me: the boy who was unafraid of feeling, who let music flow through him like water.

"Do you like this sound?" Robbie asked.

I nodded.

"Come try this one," he called out to my son. "See what you think."

For a few minutes, I watched the two of them sitting together at the keyboard, playing together.

"We don't have room for a grand," I warned.

"We'll find an upright from the same company," Robbie said. "By the way, it's Czech."

As if on cue, a salesman appeared and gave us prices for an upright. I asked for the paperwork.

"I'm going to leave tonight," Robbie said, when the salesman left. "I'll take everyone for pizza. Then I'll drive tonight and find a motel."

He was leaving. Each time still felt like a blow. I tried not to weep, but this time my son noticed.

"What's wrong?" he asked.

I told him that Robbie was going home, and that when old friends said good-bye, it made sense to feel sad.

The pizza place was noisy and it was hard to hear what anyone was saying. When we got home, my guys peeled off and Robbie and I drank some tea in our kitchen. Then he said, "Don't worry if you don't hear from me for a while. I'm not going to disappear. I hope you believe that now."

I didn't believe him, but was so filled with feelings that I couldn't speak at all.

I wheeled his suitcase out into my driveway and hoisted it into the trunk of his car. Then we stood in the dark holding one another. We didn't kiss, not on the mouth, not even on the cheek. Then Robbie got to his car and turned on the headlights. I stood just outside their glare, waiting for him to leave, but he made no move.

After a minute or two, I stepped into the glare. Back out, I ordered silently. Step on the gas and leave! For what seemed an age, he sat there. Then, finally, he drove away.

~ 28 ~

Two days later, Kate called to ask if I knew where Robbie was. I told her what he had told me: that he was headed south and would spend the night in a motel. I felt a surge of gratitude to Patrick. I always knew where he was. He always knew where I was, and that, it turned out, was essential to me.

I decided it was time to tell Patrick what I had been keeping secret from him: that I was having intrusive memories of being molested as a little girl, by my nanny's husband and that was the reason I was working with Dr. M. I waited for a quiet evening after dinner, when the kids were otherwise engaged and Patrick seemed to have nothing pressing on his mind. I explained that my memories seemed to have been activated by my work with Robbie and that I needed to continue my work with my therapist.

Patrick reacted as he did in any situation that threatened my well-being: he looked stricken, alarmed, dismayed, then posed question after logical question. Did my father know about my mother's affair? Why would a middle-aged man molest a three-year-old? Maybe I should stop writing my book? What could he do to help?

The best thing he could do, I said, was to keep on being exactly the person he was and understand that I needed to work with my doctor in private. I had confidence in Dr. M. and Patrick, whose trust in good doctors was absolute, seemed relieved and asked no more questions.

I felt sure that keeping my therapy and writing in quarantine from my family was the best way of coping with an unwelcome and unfamiliar affliction. I didn't want discussion of childhood sexual abuse to contaminate my bedroom or any other part of my house, especially since I didn't yet know what had actually happened. My mother had confirmed to me her affair with Ivan — I had recorded it in my own handwriting. I had no confirmation of his molestation of me. On the contrary, I was plagued by confusion and recurrent bouts of doubt.

I didn't, at first, tell my friends much either. How could I have been molested in my own home by the husband of my beloved nanny? The fact that it had taken place in Czech made it even less intelligible. Which of my friends could understand it and help me grasp it?

I couldn't predict their reactions or my response to them. Empathy rattled me because it made the abuse feel all too real at a time when I was not yet ready to accept it. Disbelief rattled me even more. I had been analyzed, hadn't I? How had the analyst missed this? I was devastated when one friend asked if I had proof, and reminded me that, under law, Ivan was innocent until proven guilty. I was deeply grateful to a friend who happened to be a family court judge. She never asked me for proof. Instead, she told me about a recent malpractice case in which a four-year-old girl testified that her doctor "peed" in her mouth. My friend believed her.

Having friends in positions of authority who believed me was extremely helpful. I could question those who were in the mental health professions about amnesia and recovered memory, and why they thought my memories of childhood molestation had emerged as a consequence of writing about adolescence.

They said that I might never find out: different people remembered different kinds of childhood trauma at different times and ages. A face, a smell, a tone of voice reminded them of a grandfather, uncle, cousin, or older brother or sister who had molested them. Some retained clear memories. Others were, like me, unsure of the details. Some told a parent and some parents had intervened; others had not told anyone.

A few of my friends told me, now that I had broached the subject, that they themselves had been molested as children. They were familiar with the terrain and helped me in ways neither Dr. M. or Patrick or Robbie could.

"In the interest of full disclosure," a woman who had once been my student said, "when you started telling me about your out-of-body experience, every bell in my head went off. I wanted to ask you about sexual abuse but didn't want to open something that would be hard for you to hear if you weren't ready."

Students, she reminded me, were always observing their professors and speculating about them. I had been the only female professor in our journalism department then and by far the youngest on the faculty. She had often speculated about why I seemed interested in students with difficulties, why I was so alert to abusive language in class, and why I had felt obligated to come to work the day after my father's funeral. "Now you're saying what happened to you as a child was minor compared to other people. Well, I'd like to know what you mean by minor and why you speak of it in those terms. Was it minor because you really didn't matter? Was it minor because it happened only once? What?"

I drew a blank. I couldn't answer.

"Take another look at the story you've told yourself all these years," she said. "See if it has holes. You taught me reporting. Report on yourself."

~ 29 ~

As a journalism professor, I had taught my students to observe closely, research thoroughly, then synthesize their findings and transform them into a story. When it came to my own story, though, I was unable to do most of that. I wasn't sure whether I had observed things or whether I made them up. The only way I could research anything was to interview people who knew my family about their memories. Whatever I gleaned or remembered remained in vivid but disconnected chunks.

My oldest vivid memory of sexual behavior dated from the time I was eight or nine. I had gone sledding after school with my friend Judy in a city park with a small incline. We had been sledding down and trudging back up for a while before we noticed a man in a trench coat beckoning in the twilight. We followed him to a street-level window of a red brick apartment building called the Schwab House. There were white blinds in the window, shut tight. He told us to wait there. We waited until a light went on and the blinds lifted. We watched the man take off his coat. We watched him lie down on a bed beneath a lamp. I don't remember what we saw before we turned and ran, dragging the sled behind us.

Judy had the kind of child's bedroom featured in home decoration magazines of the time: filled with pastel pillows and matched furniture that included a desk covered with multiple art supplies. I don't remember consciously setting out to make a penis, but I assembled a fistful of long colored pencils, bound them together with a rubber band, and was covering my creation with a layer of tissues that I was planning to secure with a second rubber band when Judy's mother walked in.

She was an American divorcee, whose hair and make-up made her look like one of my mother's customers. I remember her standing in the doorway staring at me in consternation. That's where my memory disintegrates. Did she scream Stop? Did she think I was about to try my phallic construction on her daughter? Did she call my mother? Did I tell her any of what had happened?

I had, over the years, tried to locate Judy and failed. When I was ready to give up, a mutual friend put us in touch. When I asked Judy if she remembered anything about sledding near the Schwab House, she quickly gave me her own account of the afternoon. It matched mine in every detail. Judy added that her maid had served us hot chocolate when we got home. Her mother may have called mine; she was dramatic in ordinary circumstances. Judy had always been an artist: she remembered the color of the man's pants. But she had more pressing problems to deal with, and did not wish to revisit negative events from her childhood.

New York was dangerous in the 1950s and 60s, I reminded Dr. M. when I told him about Judy. He remained silent and I grew more certain than ever that, unlike Robbie and me, he had grown up in some rural place where exhibitionistic men were reported and immediately apprehended. The place *I* grew up in had been dangerous, I explained to him. The West Side wasn't the rich, fashionable area it was to become. It was dilapidated, filled with gangs as well as solitary men who loitered in stairwells and lobbies and on the stoops of brownstones. Not to speak of Central Park! The Park was deserted except for lone men, some wearing trench coats. Even in 2001, when joggers flooded the old bicycle paths and the Nature Conservancy had transformed the park into a large garden, I still saw them. Didn't he?

"They're hardly likely to come on to me," Dr. M. said and I heard that as a dismissal of what was real for me.

"I'm not making this up," I argued. At reunions of my all-girls' high school, I had interviewed my high school classmates about what we considered small-time infractions — it would not have occurred to us to use the term "sexual assaults." Many had been groped by strangers on the bus or subway, by men opening their raincoats or unzipping their flies, or pressing up against them during rush hour, masturbating. *They* corroborated my experience. So did Robbie — without my needing to argue my point. Why didn't Dr. M.?

On the other hand, I defended my analyst, Robbie was nowhere near as steady and regularly available as Dr. M. Nothing about my interactions with Robbie since he drove me home from chorus rehearsal had been regular or regulated. He sent me an email or two or ten when the spirit moved him, with an innocuous question such as "Do you remember any of the Labovitz students besides me?" Or he would pose questions for which I had no easy answer, such as "What do you think caused the break between us in 1976?" We still talked the way we had for as long as I had known him — in snatches or for hours at a time, and then not for weeks or months. And, usually, it was *his* stream of consciousness that I scrambled to follow. I was unaware of the many ways in which Dr. M. was not only replacing Robbie as my most intimate collaborator, but shifting my attention to myself instead of to my partner.

Other vivid childhood incidents involving sex floated into consciousness as I tracked what came to my mind. I had been an avid reader who, by age nine, had started reading the novels my parents read. One of them was *Peyton Place,* by Grace Metalious, then the best-selling novel of the 20th century. It was easy to confirm the year of publication as 1956 and find the pages that impressed me so strongly that I persuaded my fifth-grade classmate Laura to act them out with me.

Peyton Place was a long book filled with sociological detail. I zeroed in on a short but intricate scene of sexual passion. Betty agrees to go "parking" with Rodney at night at Silver Lake. Sitting in the car, Betty dares Rodney to go swimming naked. She throws off her clothes and runs into the lake. Rodney does the same, assuming he'll catch up with her. Betty eludes him in and manages to get back into the car and into her clothes. She honks the horn and Rodney staggers up the beach naked. When he's in front of the car, she turns on the headlights. Rodney freezes like a startled deer and covers his penis with his hands. He calls Betty a bitch.

The sex-on-the-beach that follows and Betty's subsequent pregnancy were of no interest to me as a nine-year-old. I was focused on acting and re-enacting the headlights scene over and over again, with attention to exact detail and dialogue, taking turns being Betty and Rodney. I thought what we were doing was secret and wrong but somehow necessary. For years, I felt guilty for persuading Laura to do it, thinking I had caused her harm and, as I had done with Judy, I had tried over the years to locate her with no success. When I finally did a decade later, she confirmed the details of our *Peyton Place* play-acting afternoons but, unlike me, had never been troubled by them.

~ 30 ~

When I brought these memories into session, Dr. M. asked if I remembered masturbating. Most children did.

"No," I replied. "When I babysat, I sometimes saw kids do it. But I don't remember that I did."

"Would someone have stopped you?"

Impossible to ascertain, I thought, but none of the Czech adults with their anti-Puritan views were candidates.

For whatever reasons, I hadn't learned to masturbate until graduate school. It was in the Columbia Journalism library that a classmate and I had come across an issue of the feminist weekly *Off Our Backs.* The open pages featured a masturbation manual in comic strip form, with diagrams of female anatomy and a bibliography. In the spirit of the time, my classmate and I confessed our ignorance, read the recommended books (*The Sensuous Woman by J* was one), and compared our momentous experiences of do-it-yourself orgasms.

Discovering a book of recipes to "self-pleasure" at the age of 23 was like being let loose in a candy store with money to spend. The instruction to create my own sexual fantasies was as useful as the diagrams. It had not occurred to me to fantasize or to view romantic episodes in books or movies as ingredients with which to produce erotic pleasure in my own body. In retrospect, I suppose that repeatedly re-enacting pages from *Peyton Place* with Laura was a form of fantasy but our play had less to do with physical sensation for me and more with trying to find the meaning of a dramatic scene in which a girl surprised and embarrassed a naked boy.

In those early analytic sessions, I was selective in what I told Dr. M. I withheld a great deal — consciously and probably unconsciously too. I didn't, for example, reveal that I had once masturbated and had a massive orgasm in the bathroom of my mother's apartment while she was fitting a customer down the hall in her *salon.* In retrospect, I think that would have opened up a valuable network of associations, but I did not yet trust Dr. M. enough with this kind of information. Even at the time, I had wondered at my choice of time and place, but I didn't wonder whether it echoed or harkened back to anything else.

I did tell my analyst about another unusual episode from my early twenties. As a young freelancer, I pitched a spoof of *Cosmopolitan* Magazine to a journalism review. My spoof mocked its sexualized language, italics and suggestive ellipses as well as content. My editors — all men — were enthusiastic about the piece and decided to illustrate it with a full-page photograph that mimicked *Cosmo*'s weekly full-page ad on the back page of the *New York Times* business section: a sultry model with deep *décolletage* — with a typed caption of vacuous musings, ending with, *I love that magazine! I guess you could say I'm that Cosmopolitan girl!* They asked me to pose for the photograph.

At first, I told Dr. M. I was too excited by the prospect of being published to realize what being photographed by a professional photographer would entail. I wasn't aware that the *Cosmo* photograph with captions was similar to Ivan's photographs with captions. And it wasn't until I met the photographer, an intense dark-haired man in a studio with a flash-bulb camera, white umbrellas, pulsing music and hot lights, that I got cold feet. A woman told me to take off my bra, and handed me a halter-top. Then, without asking, she pushed my breasts up and together, taping them into place with duct tape.

I had burst into tears and asked her to stop.

She asked if she had hurt me with her scissors. I shook my head but said I changed my mind and didn't want to be photographed. She told her boss, who phoned my editor, who asked to talk to me.

I couldn't articulate what had so upset me but pleaded with him to let me stop. He listened, then told me what it had cost to schedule the shoot and what an unusual, attention-getting piece it would be. In the end, my desire to be published won out over my distress. My article did make a splash as did the full-page photograph of me as a *Cosmo* writer in 1973.

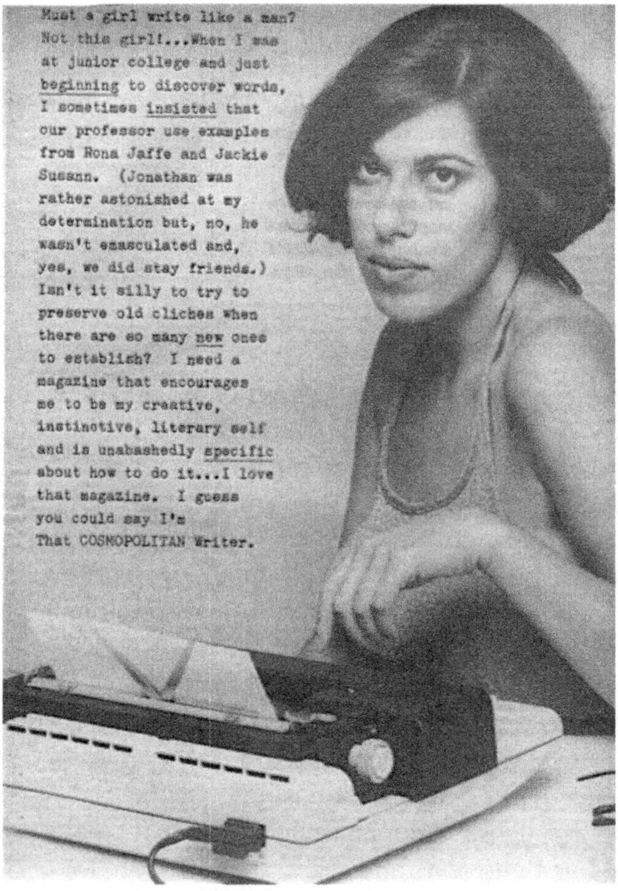

Now, 30 years later, I sent a photocopy to Dr. M. Dimly, I understood there had been a connection between the slick photographer and Ivan. But I didn't say it. I wanted my analyst to demonstrate to me how the memory of childhood trauma kept recurring in my life as an adult.

He didn't. Instead, Dr. M. wondered aloud what I had meant to convey. By 21st century standards, the photograph no longer looked provocative, but ordinary — teenage girls now wore similar halter-tops to school. You couldn't see any cleavage. In fact, the image was relatively chaste.

I tried to explain that it wasn't the photograph itself that bothered me but couldn't articulate the layers of complicated and invasive experience behind it. Or my feelings about photographs themselves — that what you see isn't always the best document of what happened.

Dr. M. didn't get what I didn't explain. He asked what message I might have been trying to send *him* with this photograph. It had nothing to do with him, I thought. I was trying to explain something that had happened to *me.* Psychoanalysis is an imperfect art in the best of circumstances. My contribution to its imperfections in those first years was to consistently withhold, dilute or disguise traumatic memory.

Friends kept insisting that working over the telephone was a factor in my lack of trust and a hindrance for any therapist. Neither of us could make use of visual cues; neither of us was playing with a full deck. So I made an effort to travel to New York every couple of months for an in-person session.

Each time, I was reminded of my dislike of Dr. M.'s East Side neighborhood. The lobby and the elevator of his building seemed too small; the corridor to his office too dim and narrow. Facing him, the room seemed to grow smaller and I thought of the encroaching walls of Edgar Allen Poe's *The Pit and the Pendulum.* In it, a prisoner of the Spanish Inquisition, tied to a wooden board by ropes, is trapped between a pit and a pendulum sharp as a scythe swinging slowly back and forth over his head. My unconscious certainly pulled no punches.

After a number of these visits, I forced myself to describe my claustrophobic reaction to Dr. M.

He surprised me. Instead of asking what came to mind, he asked whether I had ever looked up at his building's façade.

"No," I said, wondering where he was going with this.

"You never noticed the symbols in the stonework?"

"No."

The stonework featured a staff encircled by a snake, a symbol of medicine since the time of the Greeks.

Okay, I thought. Once again, meaningful to *him,* but not to me. Did he want me to interpret the staff, snake, and rod as a triple whammy phallic symbol? No, I thought, aware I was acting like a child, I wouldn't do that.

"You may not know this," he surprised me again, "but in the 1950s this building was an Eye, Ear and Throat hospital."

He paused. "Did you have a thought?"

"No," I said, lying.

Could his building be the hospital in which I had my tonsils taken out? In the 1950s, it had been close to the Czech neighborhood. Was I conflating my tonsillectomy and Ivan? Could a hospital employee have molested me?

The story I had been told about the circumstances of my tonsillectomy at age three and a half was that my mother had scheduled it to coincide with my younger brother's due date. Her idea had been to have a baby, and get my tonsils removed in one fell swoop. But my brother took his time arriving, the birth was difficult, and she was forced to remain in the hospital for two weeks. My father had walked back and forth between my hospital and my mother's. He was not permitted to stay with me overnight. Then I was sent to stay with Milena and Ivan.

I had recounted much of this episode to Dr. M. 20 years earlier, when I had refused to lie down on his couch. He had said then that the timing of my tonsillectomy had probably heightened my oedipal issues.

"Did you have another thought?" he asked.

“Do you think it’s possible someone could have molested me during that hospital stay?”

I’m not sure if he replied. Most of our sessions were still evaporating in my mind. What stuck were Dr. M.’s rare, formal comments that I wrote down on scraps of paper after I left his office, such as, *“The young child believes that impregnation happens through the mouth and that the baby comes out either through the belly-button or stomach or back out the mouth of the mother...”* And *“You came into adolescent sexuality with more than the usual burdens for a girl. There is no one way that teenagers resolve conflict around sexuality. People do it in their own ways.”*

~ 31 ~

Nine months into working with Dr. M. I was no longer weeping in public. In private, I did and was still experiencing choking sensations in my throat. Was I manufacturing symptoms?

I didn't ask. Unlike Robbie, Dr. M. did his best to keep his reactions hidden and never offered advice. He repeatedly took the position that I was a resourceful person, who excelled at research and interpretation. He reiterated that my dreams and associations came from my unconscious — not his. By refusing to explore their meaning, I was refusing self-knowledge.

I understood what he was saying but wished that he would act like my other doctors: give me a test, a diagnosis, and a remedy. I was for a long time unaware and unconvinced that I needed to diagnose and believe my condition by myself. I resented Dr. M.'s unwillingness to give me his diagnosis but, paradoxically, glad he didn't try to put words into my mouth.

Dr. M.'s insistence on my autonomy extended to his refusal to suggest books for me to read. My profession entailed extensive research skills, he said, so I began plowing through Freud, Ferenczi and Horney, then Winnicott, Bowlby, Phillips and Mitchell on my own, in the way I worked as a journalist. To make sure I understood the psychiatric terms, I even bought a doorstopper psychiatry textbook. If I needed more help, I consulted a psychologist friend. I rarely discussed my therapy with Robbie. I thought this was one field he knew less about than I did.

Reading answered some of my questions but raised doubts about the kind of therapy and therapist I had chosen.

"In the hysteric," I read. *"Freud argued that the memory of a passive sexual seduction in early childhood is repressed and remains like a foreign body in the unconscious until reanimated at puberty..."*

That felt accurate, even though I didn't want to think of myself as a hysteric. But Freud had then changed his mind about the reality of "passive sexual seduction." He came to believe it was fantasy. What did my analyst think? He was a classical psychoanalyst but also a child psychiatrist. Like my judge friend, he must have had first-hand experience of sexually-abused children. How did he reconcile his patients' stories with Freud's theories? Was he my ally or adversary?

Dr. M. steadfastly refused to betray any views.

"What comes to mind?" he'd say. Often, to level the playing field, I refused to say. I didn't want to play by his rules.

On the other hand, most of the time his rules helped me feel safe. I was aware of discomfort only at close quarters and sometimes over the telephone, when his voice sounded practically inside my ear. It made me wonder what he was doing.

"I can hear you breathe," was what I said.

"I have to breathe," he had replied. Sensibly, but not too helpfully, I thought. He was breathing heavily and I wanted him to explain why. A cold? Allergies? Was he chewing gum, or that most difficult thought — masturbating?

Then, swinging to his defense: he's a doctor! I didn't have to start from scratch with someone new. He was responsible for my being able to get married and have a family. Psychoanalysis might be obsolete, but it was working for me. I liked its formality and slowness. I was an athlete's daughter who knew the value of regular practice and a good coach.

But some coaches are untrustworthy, another part of me argued. Just look at the news. Asking someone who had been molested to trust her therapist, I had read in one of the best books by a therapist, was like inviting her to jump from the top of a building. That was exactly how I felt. I began to appreciate Dr. M.'s caution and the way it allowed me to control the pace of investigation.

Meanwhile, in the world outside analysis, I continued to function as a wife, mother, and public speaker. In September of 2001, I flew to a conference in Norway about war and literature, one of three women and eight male literary lions, on a small island above the Arctic Circle. The men — Arab, Israeli, South Korean, Bosnian, German, South African, Russian — described how war and political violence had shaped their lives. Feeling out-credentialed, like a child in a room of adults, I didn't mention how sexual violence had affected my writing.

No one mentioned sexual violence. It came up only once, in a twisted way, when the celebrated Soviet-era poet complained that the politically correct regime at the University of Oklahoma forced him to keep his door open during office hours. "I do not like to be greeted with Fascism," he declaimed. Was this American freedom?

"Yes," I was surprised to hear myself reply, "freedom from sexual harassment." A younger man at the dinner table backed me up but the older ones moved on to discuss how they wrote about love. I observed the Russian. His rock star affect and insinuating manner reminded me of Mick Jagger, but his Slavic accent, slick hair, and boozy smell of Ivan. I covered my distaste as we posed for photographs, smiling for the camera as he draped his arm around my shoulders. I noticed how easily I slipped into deference, taking a back seat to people I considered real survivors.

Re-entry to my family in Massachusetts that September of 2001 was the usual circus, exacerbated by jet lag. I was almost back on schedule a week later, breakfast cleared away and settling down at my desk, when I heard something on the radio about the World Trade Center. I thought it was a critic describing the plot of a movie, but when the story was taken up by other commentators, I went upstairs and turned on the TV and, while the WTC footage kept running over and over again, my body went numb.

Patrick called from Pittsburgh. He had flown out of Logan Airport — the airport that one group of terrorists had used — on business the day before. All U.S. air traffic was grounded, he said. His client was loaning him a car, and he would drive back to Massachusetts. Even though the lines to New York City were working, I couldn't get through to my brothers or my friends, or Dr. M. None of them worked near the towers and I assumed they were safe.

Of course, I thought of Robbie, watching the looping television footage out on the west coast. The World Trade Center was part of our world: we had watched its slow construction as teenagers. But I didn't call. We had argued about a racial discrimination lawsuit he was hell-bent on bringing against the university where Kate taught. I thought it was a bad idea and advised against it. Robbie had become enraged by my "lack of social consciousness" and cut off our correspondence three months before. Though 9/11 dwarfed everything, I was still angry at Robbie.

When my sons got home, they told me that the high school principal announced the disaster over the PA system. The younger one, who took a class there, had been intercepted by a policeman on his way back to his middle school, and told to keep the news from his classmates. He seemed proud rather than burdened by being entrusted with a secret.

I dialed Dr. M. at my usual hour on the next day, feeling guilty to be taking up his time with memories when the children in his waiting room had current needs. Did he know anyone who had been inside the towers? I wanted to know. How had he found out it had happened? How was he feeling?

But even 9/11 didn't dent Dr. M.'s protocols. He said, "I'm managing all right. You?" and waited for me to speak again. It wasn't my job to take care of him, I reminded myself. My job was to do the work: say whatever came to mind.

So I did. I told him how I had heard about the planes, how my reaction of numbness had reminded me of my response to the Soviet invasion of Czechoslovakia, how the ash falling from the burning buildings filled with people reminded me of the crematoria in Auschwitz, and then — out of the blue — I blurted out a secret.

I had a close friend who was having sex with her therapist, I said. Our children had met at age five. I thought of her as a sister I never had. For months I had been keeping her secret, feeling burdened by that knowledge.

"Report him," said Dr. M. immediately.

"I can't," I replied, startled by his abandoning his script. "I promised not to tell anyone."

"Look," he said, in a tone of voice I hadn't heard from him before. "Not reporting this guy is like letting a pedophile loose in a neighborhood of children. You're protecting the abuser."

Then he stopped and I heard him add — to himself, I thought — that perhaps he shouldn't have said what he did, that it might dissuade me from confiding in him in the future.

"No," I replied. "I'm glad."

That was an understatement. I was immeasurably relieved that my therapist was urging me to take action against a man who, though his professional colleague, was a sexual predator.

I wrote our exchange down in my journal. Then I forgot that I had done it. It would be several years until my friend herself reported her therapist to the state licensing board and I went back to my documentation of her confidences to provide details and dates from my journal in support of her complaint. It would take that long — several years of analysis — before I understood this psychological mechanism I employed for dealing with trauma: writing things down was, for me, a way of both recording and refusing to take in the reality of knowledge that overwhelmed me. It was a form of self-protection and deferral until I was strong enough to absorb the reality of an experience.

~ 32 ~

I rarely discussed Robbie with Dr. M., but therapy was nonetheless making me re-examine my relationships with the people I most loved. Slowly I began to see that Robbie's passion for music, ideas and causes obscured the intensity of his moods and their sudden, sometimes explosive, fluctuations. I noticed that I was still holding on to an adolescent fantasy of Robbie that made me unable to see his insecurities or his prickly defensiveness. It was difficult to amend my adulation of the man I had known since the age of 15. But I was amending it. Also, as I got deeper into working with Dr. M. I began talking to him about what I would have talked about with Robbie.

Six months after 9/11, the *Boston Globe* broke the bombshell story of the decades-long cover-up of sexual abuse of children within the Catholic Church.

I didn't have to read the installments. I heard the revelations almost daily that winter in the locker room of our community pool, from other women swimmers. Some of them were old, observant Catholics, who recognized the names of the priests and churches. Others were non-Catholics but long-time locals familiar with the hegemony of the church. Usually they chatted about books and concerts as they changed into their swimsuits, or about snow removal and black ice. I was heartened by their anger and by their support of the victims. I drank in their words: "These men of God kept the crimes secret for decades" and "those children told the truth."

By the end of 2002, over 1,000 priests had been accused of sexual abuse of children in the United States and bishops were resigning in far away South America and Europe. Discussion of sexual abuse became routine in the media. I was proud of my fellow journalists. I was encouraged by the response of the community and understood that societal changes were uncovering and validating psychic trauma. But maybe that was because the abused boys and girls were Catholic, maybe because the abusers were priests, I didn't consciously draw a parallel between those children and myself. My wish to deny and dissociate was still very strong. After I reported on the locker room discussion and *Globe* investigation to Dr. M. I didn't bring the church scandal into session again.

I began to bring in dreams. I hadn't paid much attention to my dreams before entering analysis. Now I told Patrick not to say a word in the morning so I could write them down right away. Working on dreams, I explored many associations to a single word or image, waiting for them to bob up out of my unconscious like air bubbles from water. Journalism had trained me to organize my observations in a linear fashion, tracking cause and effect. The pressure of deadlines encouraged accepting a first answer to a question as the definitive one. In session, I imitated Dr. M. in that I was silent until a thought made itself heard.

I also learned to see my dreams as films of my own making, creative products out of my conscious control. At first, I experienced my dreams as so disconnected from me that I sometimes critiqued them as though they had been made by someone else. I dismissed some as banal, was thrilled when they contained ingenious references or inventive word play. They seemed safer than conscious thoughts: I didn't feel responsible for their content.

One dream kept recurring like a nagging worry: the dream of sitting in a rooftop bathtub with my husband, and Robbie gazing down at us from another roof, like King David gazing at Bathsheba in the Old Testament. Who was standing in for whom in this dream? Was it about me and Robbie, or my mother and Ivan?

It would take years before I understood that Bathsheba was both my mother and myself; that Ivan embodied both sides of King David; that the bathtub was the place from which I watched their assignations.

I also dreamed more variations on phallic vegetables and a disembodied penis. The most eloquent one featured it lying amid the chalks and scissors on my mother's worktable. This dream was straightforward. "Penis on the table," I thought at once, was my analytic agenda. Sex had been as much the fabric of my mother's business as the actual material from which she made clothing. It was also my material as a writer.

Slowly, I learned to interpret the language of my dreams. When I dreamt I was in a taxicab in Prague with two male journalists, I remembered that most of my interviewers when I did publicity for a book there had been men. One had invited me to bed, and seemed offended when I refused. In the dream, the cab was crammed with photographic equipment and a large, wrinkled ball that looked like an enormous testicle or beach ball from Silver Point beach where Ivan had photographed my parents and me. I could identify the provenance of each item, but was unable to piece them together.

Then, as though my unconscious decided to be more explicit, I dreamt of being in another taxi with two famous opera singers. As I woke, up, someone said, "I don't know what kind of car Domingo drives but I know what Pavarotti eats."

This was very difficult for me to say out loud to Dr. M.

He waited for a while before saying, "Anything come to mind?"

"Yes," I said, startled to hear that there was a part of me that generated foul language, "Eats dick."

I hadn't thought of this episode in my professional life for a long time. One of my first assignments for the *New York Times* was a magazine profile of an opera star who insisted on teaching me how to make *fettuccine alfredo* in his apartment overlooking

Central Park. I became anxious about how this would substitute for an interview.

His agent came in with some urgent business and asked me to wait in the bedroom for a minute. I had left my notebook in the living room. Thinking I'd find pen and paper in the bedside drawer, I pulled it open. It contained a beige plastic vibrator.

Vibrators were on display in drugstore windows all over the city at the time. *The Sensuous Woman* had discussed their efficacy, yet I reacted as though I had seen a rat. What did the singer use it for? On whom? I asked like the grade schooler I had been asking the meaning of the word "fuck." When I was called back into the living room, I shut the drawer, and resumed working as though nothing was amiss. I even posed for a photograph with the singer, both of us smiling for the camera.

"Did you think he ate dick?" Dr. M. asked in his neutral tone.

I was so shocked that I lost track of the rest of the session and didn't realize he was repeating my words.

"We have to stop," was the next thing I heard and as I replaced the telephone receiver I was once again relieved that we hadn't been face-to-face. I wrote, "ate dick" in my journal. Another expression I had never understood. Who ate dick? Girls or boys? Why? Was it good or bad? And what did it say about you? I didn't ask anyone. It seemed too dangerous. Curiosity and its consequences was a mixed experience for me.

One year after sending Dr. M. my first email about Ivan coming in my mouth, I returned to a sentence I hadn't been able to complete in session at that time: "All men like blow jobs. You are a man, therefore..."

Now, with what seemed like an enormous effort of will, I was able to complete it in private, at home: "You are a man; therefore you like blow jobs."

However tame or lame that sentence, formulating it felt like an extraordinary act of courage. As soon as I had, something short-circuited in my brain.

Eventually, I began to compose a succession of simple thoughts: "You are a man; therefore you like blow jobs" meant that Dr. M. was another Ivan or Robbie, who would make fun of me, as Robbie had by telling his dirty jokes. He would think that I refused to perform blow jobs or have oral sex. Or that I enjoyed but disowned it. Either way, I didn't want to get into a conversation about this with Dr. M. — not in person or over the telephone.

I tried to utilize what I had read about "disorganized" and "dissociated" contents of a child's mind that stayed intact through adulthood. Especially scary were the parts that came to me in Czech. To "offend" in Czech, was *urázit,* a recurrent, important word in my upbringing, applied in different ways to adults and children. It was impolite to offend an adult and impolite for me, a child, to show or say that I had been offended. If I acted *urážená,* the adults would make fun of me.

There was more. Since Dr. M. was a man, he might ask me to give him a blow job. I would offend him if I refused. He would go away and I would be left alone. Had I been able to access my adult mind, I might have understood that I believed Dr. M. might either assault me or abandon me if I refused to go along with his wishes. Assault, I wrote in my journal, meant, "to be forced down to your knees and have a stiff penis pry open your mouth cutting off oxygen, suffocating and choking you."

I could say none of this to Dr. M.

Instead I told him another episode from my early twenties, during one of those periods when Robbie was absent from my life and I was able to notice and be attracted to other men. A friend took me to visit an Israeli peace activist whose floating radio station broadcast rock music into warring Middle Eastern countries. The man had docked his ship in New York to raise money and my friend thought I should interview him.

I was a very inexperienced journalist back then, awed by the moment. As we sat on deck, looking at the Manhattan skyline and talking, I could pick out my parents' Riverside Drive apartment building across the water. I also noticed that the activist was twice my age and spoke English with a foreign accent. In retrospect, I see that he looked a lot like Ivan.

The next day I went back with a tape recorder to interview him. He was a war hero committed to peace. In pursuit of that elusive goal, he had flown an Israeli plane into Egypt when the border was closed. He had airlifted food to starving children in Africa. And he had his radio station. I enjoyed his stories. When my tape recorder clicked to a stop, he proposed we go to his cabin.

I was flattered by the attention of a famous man. We had sex in a berth of his Captain's Cabin. That was new but I was still not feeling much and wondering why I didn't have orgasms with men the way I did by myself.

When it was over, the peace activist asked me to return the next day because he had more to tell me.

I took the bait. I came back with my tape recorder, he talked for the duration of my second tape cassette, and then again invited me to his cabin. This time, he pushed me down into the narrow space on the floor and forced his penis into my face. I don't remember feeling anything but surprise. I don't remember protesting or doing anything at all until he came in my mouth. I gagged and wiped it off with the back of my hand.

I made an effort to describe this whole episode as best I could to Dr. M. in a phone session but it was excruciating. I self-censored and left out key details. I asked if "glucous" was a word, but didn't explain that I thought semen looked like glue and mucous mixed, and that it tasted salty, like cucumbers with salt. I didn't say that cucumbers were among the phallic vegetables I had been dreaming about and that I had had an odd habit as a teenager of eating whole cucumbers with salt — to the amusement of my friends. Most important, I wasn't able to explain what seems obvious in retrospect — that the activist was a political hero and radio broadcaster who resembled Ivan down to his fondness for whiskey. I was so vague that Dr. M. did not recognize a re-enactment.

The only thing he asked was why I had gone back to the ship after I had gotten my story.

Because I was young and stupid? I thought angrily. Because I had never before met a guy with a peace ship? Dr. M. seemed to be implying that I had invited oral rape. What I took to be his obtuseness ended our session.

My girlfriends had no trouble understanding why, at 24, I had gone back to the peace ship. They also pointed out that my quest for sexual experience as a young woman was not to be conflated with my molestation as a little girl. Though I might have been curious as a toddler, I couldn't be held responsible for whatever had happened. "The child is in an impossible situation," I wrote in my journal after talking to one friend. "If I don't play along, I lose Milena AND I lose my mother. It's like checkmate."

I didn't, at the time, even notice my unconscious punning on the word Czech.

In part because I was discouraged by trying to communicate with my analyst in words, I started sending Dr. M. drawings of my dreams, thinking we might have better luck with images both of us could see. When his assistant revealed that he was also a child psychiatrist, I had imagined myself being able to draw instead of talk or to do play therapy, like Dibs, the boy in *DIBS: In Search of Self,* the classic book about a therapy with a deeply troubled little boy by his dedicated female therapist.

I had never even doodled before but now I bought a sketchbook and water colors and began trying to record some of my dreams. When an image was relatively easy to draw, like a Christmas candle melting wax into a child's palm, I drew it myself. If I thought it was hard to get right — a pitcher of milk pouring liquid into my face, for instance — I asked an artist friend if she could draw it for me.

Since Robbie's visit to my home, I had also been poring over photographs. In a movie popular during my adolescence, a photographer studied image after image, looking for evidence of some kind. I couldn't remember why he was looking, but it involved sex and death.

I decided to mail Dr. M. a photograph Ivan had taken in his living room apartment when I was about seven.

Perusing it as I had watched Robbie do, I noted my bare knees and thighs, the way my skirt has hiked up and the ambiguous expression — surprise at being interrupted as I read my book? fear? — on my face. I recognize the fabric of my skirt made from a customer's remnants and the fabric of the couch and pillow in Milena and Ivan's apartment.

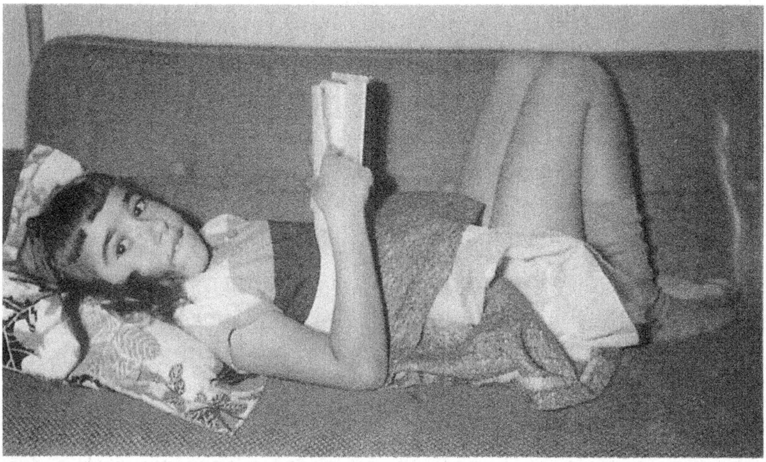

Before I emailed the photograph to Dr. M. I had sent it to a photographer friend, asking only for her opinion of the picture.

"Looks like child porn," she answered.

When I asked my analyst the same question, he said, "Nice photograph of you as a little girl."

Was he joking? Was he bending over backwards not to resemble a therapist accused of planting ideas in children's minds after the day-care abuse trials of the 1980s? How could he not see what was plain to me? He was acting as obtusely as my father!

Who was he anyway? I had been referred to him two decades earlier; who knew what he had done since? He could have become an axe murderer for all I knew. He didn't speak my language or share my point of view. I had trusted him, doubled the number of my sessions, divulged my dreams, and anxiety about his heavy breathing. How did I even know he was a *bona fide* analyst? I hadn't asked him any questions!

I went online to check him out.

In a few minutes, I went from knowing almost nothing about Dr. M. to knowing a great deal: where he had grown up (I had been right about the far away), where he had been trained as a doctor, where he had worked. I read papers he had written and opinions on children and adolescents that reporters had quoted. My most unexpected and important hit was an unpublished manuscript in a university archive written by his father. Dr. M. was, like me, a child of Holocaust survivors!

That explained his incongruous chuckle when, at our very first session, I had given him a tutorial on the effects of the war and how they made it difficult to separate from my mother.

I read the manuscript from beginning to end, satisfying years of curiosity. Far from being a stranger to my background, my analyst was like part of an extended family.

This raised many questions in my mind. He had moved far away from his parents early on: had he found separation easier than I had? Did he look down on me for not having been able to do what he had? He must have read my book about inter-generational transmission of Holocaust trauma: what had he thought?

His parents had a very different history from my parents. His were Lithuanians. They had fallen in love before the war, with a proper courtship, wedding, honeymoon, and two daughters born before the war! They had managed to keep their family alive and together at first. Then their luck ran out: one daughter was rounded up and murdered. Another was hidden and had survived the war.

Reading my analyst's father's memoir introduced new complications into my already complicated feelings toward Dr. M. Instead of seeing him as far away, he was now extremely close, and a peer rather than a parent surrogate. I wondered how he had integrated his family background. His subset of European Jews were considered super-rational, arrogant snobs whose culture might explain his assumption that my parents valued boys more than girls. Also his surprise at my family's casual attitudes toward nudity, marriage and sex. In his father's account, my analyst seemed to be the quintessential Jewish prince: the Doctor!

I wondered if his feelings toward me were colored by his complicated relationships to his sisters, one dead, one living; he so often emphasized the importance of siblings. What were his loyalties to them, to his parents, to himself and, by extension, to me?

I didn't formulate those questions as clearly then as now. I was confused, excited, and anxious. Why did I feel like a stalker? I had suddenly discovered what I wasn't supposed to know. Was that my fault? It was public information. Anyone could go on the internet. I was a journalist as well as an analysand. Was I allowed to investigate my therapist or not? The speed of going from knowing nothing to everything shocked me, as did my sense of having done something deeply wrong. I had looked at something I was not supposed to look at. I knew what I was not meant to know.

Aware that I was adopting the language of the Church, I thought: I have to confess my transgression.

~ 33 ~

I steeled myself and said: "I looked you up online and found your father's memoir. I read the whole thing."

The pause. Then — did I detect amusement? — "Well, what did you think?"

I thought I was glad we weren't face to face. I thought: thank God for analytic protocol. I thought the contents of the memoir paled beside the enormity of my having read it. I had bitten off more than I could chew. The Apple: New York. The forbidden fruit of the tree of knowledge in Sunday School. Eating dick. I would be punished. I had bitten another child in nursery school. The collage of red lips over white teeth in the album Ivan had made for Franci. Curiosity killed the cat and might kill me. I wasn't supposed to know about the murder of Dr. M.'s sister or Dr. M.'s date of birth. How could I say that I had looked up the compatibility of his astrological sign with mine?

But he had asked what I thought of the memoir and I monitored my chain of associations, editing out anything I thought might offend him. I couldn't find words to express my horror at his sister's murder and how it had affected him as the child who was born after her death. I was afraid to comment on his parents or point out how different his wily father had been from mine. Instead, I decided to talk about the similarities between our fathers. They were middle-class men of the same generation, with no preparation for the catastrophe that overtook them. They expressed themselves plainly, relied on dates and numbers in their accounts. Both had been born into privilege and lost that position in war and emigration. Both had been obliged to rely on their smart, enterprising wives.

I didn't share any of my questions, such as: what kind of parent had his father been? Had he exhibited my father's sudden rages or absent-minded moods? How old had Dr. M. been when his parents told him about the murder of his sister and other episodes from the war? Had he learned to dissociate while he listened as I had? Did that help or hinder him in his work? Did he view his sister who survived as a heroine? Did he expect me to emulate her?

I remember babbling about the thousands of people I had met while researching Holocaust survivors, emphasizing how unusual his family was, and how lucky in that three of them had survived. The one thing I clearly remember was my sentence, "If we're going to go scuba diving together, we better take along a lot of oxygen." Associations: swimming, shared breathing, coral reefs, adventure, mutual dependence, and the possibility of drowning underwater.

Considering Dr. M.'s two older sisters reminded me that I had two younger brothers whom I had not spent much time discussing. Unlike my analyst, I was a first-born child; siblings had not played as consequential a role in my life as they had in his. My brothers were both skiers. Neither was a reader and we rarely discussed books, including the ones I wrote. I had been nearly 13 years old when David was born; three and a half, when Tommy arrived. For a long time, I identified more with our parents and their interests than with them and theirs.

That changed when our parents died and when my brothers and I had children. Though Tommy and I were three and a half years apart in age and had very different temperaments and friends, I realized he had been my earliest ally and the sole living witness to my early childhood. Unlike me, he was quiet and introspective, a one-time art student who now supervised the construction of large city buildings. Every once in a while, when I came into the city to see Dr. M. we had lunch or dinner together. When he sat at the table facing me — a well-dressed man, graying at the temples — I always thought of our mother. While she and I looked so alike it was hard to identify who was who in photographs, my mother and brother shared less obvious traits: an interest in clothes and depressive temperaments.

My brother had helped me on my first book; now, both of us middle-aged, I was curious what he thought of our parents' marriage.

"They were both overwhelmed," he said. "Kurt was a fish out of water in America but he was no fool — he was the one who got them out of Czechoslovakia. But he didn't speak the language and he never adapted. He coped with his sports discipline — got up early in the morning, took his cold shower, went to work. He was a happier person than Mom."

That was a perceptive summary of our father, I thought and, emulating Dr. M. kept silent.

My brother continued, "She was urban, cultured, had the languages, could do the crossword puzzle. But she was frustrated in her work, had the stress of running the business, plus medical problems plus her psychological issues.

"They were gifted in different areas but they did everything together. I didn't think they'd ever get divorced, the way I thought she might kill herself."

Yes, I thought, waited, and then asked, "Do you remember any of their friends? Ivan and Milena?"

"Of course. They were like grandparents. Milena was like a saint. Everybody loved her. Ivan always seemed like a man capable of anything."

"Did you know that he and Mom had an affair?"

My brother looked at me as though I was crazy. "When?"

"When we were kids."

"I meant *when could she have an affair?* Mom and Dad were always together. And when they weren't together, she was working. She never left the house."

"She went out every day," I said evenly, emulating Dr. M. "Food shopping, to the bank, to the fabric stores; to all her doctors. To the opera and concerts — usually without Daddy."

My brother looked so incredulous that I didn't point out what had become obvious to me: that our mother hadn't left home to have sex with Ivan. They did it in our apartment.

"How did this come up?" my brother asked.

I told him that I was working on a new book and that Robbie — whom my brother remembered well — was helping me. In the course of our conversations I remembered that Franci divulged her affair the day before I began analysis "to save me time."

"That sounds right," my brother said, half laughing. "In her mind, it was no big deal. You always had the sense that nothing after the war was a big deal. Nothing was a tragedy. Their tragedy was behind them."

Not a tragedy — those were the words Franci had used when I was upset about something that she deemed negligible.

Now my brother was saying the same thing.

We had grown up hearing about the customers' affairs over dinner and, after Kurt died, leaving Franci a 55-year-old widow, she had a couple of open affairs — one with a married man — of which she made no secret. I had felt uncomfortable with both men, but neither of my brothers expressed dismay. Was I being puritanical or did meeting my mother's lovers revive acute childhood memories?

I didn't feel comfortable enough with my brother to tell him that Ivan had molested me. My brother was a private man, uncomfortable with my writing about our family. His reactions to my questions seemed to me tinged with disbelief and distaste and threw me into uncertainty.

Robbie remained the person with whom I felt most comfortable talking about it all. A couple of weeks after 9/11 we had resumed our long conversation as though it had never been interrupted. I called him up and described the despair I felt about ever being able to believe what had happened. I told Robbie that I had tracked down Ivan's son in California and interrogated him about his father. He had been helpful and forthcoming with information about Ivan. He had sent me a long letter, answering every question I asked and describing his father as an important political journalist and prominent figure in the Czech community. It was clear why my mother had been attracted to him, but not at all clear why he would have molested me. All my doubts returned: did it happen? if it happened, is it really a big deal in the greater scheme of things?

Robbie listened until he lost patience, then blurted, "I have no doubt that it happened. It's like a detective story. I knew this was where it was going — there were so many clues. Your experience was as terrifying as anything they went through. What's it going to take for you to feel you can have a right to your own life? A tattoo?"

It felt good to hear Robbie say this with his customary passion, but I didn't think my experience was as terrifying as anything my parents or Ivan had gone through. I did repeat to myself the rest of what he said though I didn't completely take it in.

I understood Robbie to mean: did I have to be victimized in equal measure to my mother before I felt I had a right to complain?

No one could corroborate my memories of molestation except Ivan, Robbie argued. Ivan was long dead. So what was I after? I couldn't answer that question. All I knew was that I felt compelled to gather yet more evidence to convince me to believe that what I knew was true.

~ 34 ~

Of all the books I read to understand my state of mind, Judith Herman's *Trauma and Recovery* made the most sense to me. The study of trauma, she wrote, has a curious history of recurrent amnesia. Not only individuals, but entire societies alternated between periods of remembering and periods of forgetting. It seemed it was too painful for human beings to retain the memory of psychic injury.

But, paradoxically, traumatic events, collective or individual, refuse to be buried. *"Equally as powerful as the desire to deny atrocities is the conviction that denial will not work,"* Herman wrote. *"The dialectic of trauma gives rise to complicated, sometimes uncanny alterations of consciousness, which George Orwell, one of the committed truth-tellers of our century, called 'doublethink,' and which mental health professionals, searching for a calm, precise language, call 'dissociation.'"*

Judith Herman had been trained as a physician. She was a feminist and, even before her training as a psychiatrist was complete, had come into contact with patients who had been sexually abused. Her ability to integrate history, medicine, psychology, feminism, and literature became indispensable to me: she explained why I had been unable to integrate my own experiences of trauma, made them cohere.

I read and underlined and reread *Trauma and Recovery.* Then, I discovered that Judith Herman taught a trauma seminar at

Harvard Medical School, not far from where I lived. I wrote her to ask if I might audit.

Since I had written a book about the inter-generational transmission of psychic trauma, no one questioned why I was at the seminar table. Week after week, I sat between a psychiatric nurse and a child psychologist listening to a wide variety of guest lecturers discuss cases, results of research studies, and various approaches to treating trauma.

Shame, secrecy, and silence were the deadly trio that prolonged and abetted the effects of trauma, I heard. That trio was often enacted by the abuser, the bystanders, the victim, or all three. I was all too aware of my own silence and secrecy as I sat at the seminar table. I was only beginning to be aware of feeling shame, considering how often I had been disparaged and disparaged myself through the examples offered by the cases we studied. I filled a special notebook with pithy quotes, including: *"The root of trauma is when the child cries out and no one is there."*

Shame, secrecy, and silence, Dr. Herman argued, were often rendered inoperative when trauma was experienced collectively. Everyone in our seminar room and our country had experienced such an event during the World Trade Center attack on 9/11. There was no doubt about its reality. It was witnessed, documented, and validated in hundreds of public ways. Yet even such public, collective trauma could be cloaked by shame, as in mass rape of women or genocide.

But trauma experienced by one person, in private, had a very different context. It was characterized by the absence of witnesses and validators and, often, the inability of the victim to put his or her experience into words. One day Dr. Herman showed slides of paintings and drawings, artworks that expressed what some of her clients could not or would not articulate in words. One was a watercolor of a girl's disembodied head floating in the sky. As I sat in the darkened room at the table of students of trauma, I thought about how lucky I was to have found the perfect complement to my work with Dr. M.: a cognitive therapy where I was an invisible patient.

I listened to experts describe people who cut off feeling from fact when traumatized; people who had auditory or visual or tactile memories of the event; severely traumatized people who often drifted into "fugue states," during which their sense of body, time, place, speech or hearing disappeared entirely; people who coped by developing multiple personalities, called "dissociative identity disorders."

I recognized myself on the lower end of the dissociative spectrum of behavior. I easily lose a sense of time and place while driving or writing or listening to music. My friends sometimes pointed out to me that I was behaving as though I had just learned something for the first time when, in fact, they remembered me telling them about it years before. My mind was, I realized, like the Magic Slate I had adored playing with as a child. I wrote a sentence. I lifted the page. The words became invisible: they vanished. I had a very good memory for other people's stories; a problematic one for my own.

The term that spoke most directly to me was "splitting." I connected it to one of the most graphic stories my mother told me about Auschwitz. After her hair was shaved off and her forearm was tattooed with a number, she had experienced the curious sensation of looking down at that forearm and watching it divide into two arms. Then her entire body had become two bodies. She told me that for the rest of the war, one of her had watched the other. Listening to the seminar lecturers describe "dissociation as defense," I wondered whether my mother's capacity to dissociate was in my DNA, or whether it was learned behavior.

I had split into two bodies in a similar way during the Soviet invasion of Czechoslovakia, and when I shot out of my body and watched another me have sex with Robbie, and when, years before, I took mescaline. Also when I had a miscarriage. I sat in a hospital room looking down as a bowl filled slowly with my blood. Patrick was with me, weeping; my vital signs were being closely monitored by nurses, and though I was thinking I might bleed to death, I felt absolutely nothing.

At times, that dissociative reaction was useful but often, it was not. It was as though I had learned over the years to perform involuntary, unconscious psychological triage. Before I was aware of what I saw or felt, I selected whether to retain or forget it.

Lecturer after lecturer in Dr. Herman's seminar pointed to the many extra-therapeutic factors that helped or hindered awareness of such defenses and recovery from traumatic events: family, friends, community, class, political and religious attitudes and cultural traditions. All had significant impact, in some cases as much or more than psychotherapy. I don't remember that anyone mentioned the importance of a supportive partner or being unconditionally loved.

Psychoanalysis fared poorly in the trauma seminar: it was disparaged as obsolete, expensive, patriarchal. That worried me and sharpened my scrutiny of Dr. M. One week I thought I should quit. Another week, I realized how helpful it was, and how steadying. Then, Dr. M.'s phone line would be busy when I called. Once, twice, three times. I would check my calendar and double-check the time to make sure I was not mistaken. Then I'd get angry that he was not available at our designated time but was afraid to tell him.

"Are you stage-managing this?" I asked after our wires crossed several times.

"No," he replied directly for once. "I wouldn't do that."

"Why not?"

"It would be bad technique, not conducive to trust."

Good answer, I thought, but wondered if it were true.

I wanted him to know all that Dr. Herman did but when I asked whether he had read her book he said, "No," and suggested that I mail him pages I found important. I told him the whole book was important. How could he not have read it? Was he dyslexic? Sexist? One of those docs who never read anything but professional journals? Who knew.

All I knew was that I had come to Dr. M. as a shipwreck. My ballast had failed and I had needed righting. Now I was sailing in the storm, and I believed that the practice of psychoanalysis kept me going. I had practiced many disciplines before — music, sports, writing — and knew the importance of time and routine for eventual pay-off. Despite my evasions and self-censoring, I told more to Dr. M. than to anyone else. He knew what I kept secret from most of the world. I trusted him to keep it private in that odd container called a "session." I knew he'd try to withhold his own reactions and keep track of my disclosures until I could tolerate discussing them in depth.

That was my thinking in the summer of 2003, when I was at my lakeside cottage alone just after a flash flood. I had stood by the window watching the water, amazed by its power and how, when it ended, the water soaked into the ground and it was as though nothing had happened. I called Dr. M. at our usual time, described the sudden scary rush of water and then stopped dead.

"Anything come to mind?" Dr. M. asked.

"The waterfall out west with Robbie," I said. "And going out on the rock jetty when I was a little kid."

Suddenly, I imagined his face morphing the way it had done the first time I saw him in person. This time, two years into our work, I was able to tell him what I was seeing and feeling as it was happening.

"I'm embarrassed to say this, but I'm seeing your head turning into the head of a wolf."

Then I stopped, appalled at what I had said.

"Go on," said Dr. M. as though he heard this kind of thing all the time.

I took a breath. "I'm going to visit my grandmother... I'm going through the woods to my grandmother's house."

I stopped again. Why was I telling my shrink the story of Little Red Riding Hood? He was a child psychiatrist! He surely knew it. Then I realized I no longer did. I couldn't remember what happened. That was terrifying. How could I not know the story of Little Red?

"You're going through the woods." Dr. M. reminded me.

"I'm at my grandmother's house," I said, aware that I was in my own cottage in Massachusetts, talking to my analyst. How could I be in two places at once?

"Is she there?" I heard Dr. M. ask through the telephone receiver as though this was a normal conversation.

"No," I replied, hearing my voice as in a dream. "She's not there." And I stopped again.

"Is anybody there?" Dr. M. asked.

There didn't seem to be. Something had happened to ordinary time. It, too, had stopped.

"Is anybody there?" Dr. M. asked again.

"I don't know," I said, embarrassed. I was inside the story I had read hundreds of times, by myself, to dozens of children for whom I had babysat. I scanned my brain, prompting it with keywords: Red. Riding. Hood. Nothing.

"Do you want me to tell you?"

"Yes," I finally said.

"The wolf is there."

"The wolf is there," I repeated blankly. Why was the wolf there? I felt stupid, the way in fifth grade I had felt stupid when I didn't know the meaning of the word "fuck."

"You don't remember," said Dr. M. after a pause.

"No," I said. I couldn't for the life of me remember what happened next.

"They have a conversation."

A conversation? What kind of conversation could she have had with a wolf?

"She says 'Grandma, what big eyes you have!'" Dr. M. said quietly.

In a flash, I was back in my body. I knew this sequence of dialogue!

"The better to see you with," I replied. That was what the wolf had said. Then Little Red said, "Grandmother, what big hands you have!" and the wolf had replied, "The better to hold you with!" Then "Grandmother, what big teeth you have!"

Then "The better to eat you all up!" Then the wolf, had leaped out of bed and eaten her.

There was a long silence and then I was surprised to hear myself say "I don't have a grandmother. My pretend grandmother is Milena and I'm going to visit her. But I'm not in the woods; I'm in New York City and I can't go to her house alone."

I stopped again.

"Someone took me." I felt a stab in my chest and, silently, I began to weep. "My father. My father's taking me to my grandmother's house."

Another pause. "Of course he doesn't know what's going to happen."

Then, "I know why he's taking me there," I said, the words coming out in a rush. "He's going to see my mother who's in the hospital having my baby brother and kids aren't allowed in the hospital so he's taking me to stay with Milena. But when we get there, she's not there..."

I stopped talking again.

"Do you remember how the story ends?" Dr. M. finally broke in. I tried to think. Little Red Riding Hood was in the wolf's belly with her grandmother. How did they get out? The answer seemed unfathomable. "I don't know," I said, finally giving up trying to find the answer. "Will you tell me?"

"No," said my analyst calmly. "You're a resourceful person — you can look it up! We have to stop now."

As soon as I hung up with Dr. M., I dialed a lawyer friend and begged her to write down everything I told her: how the flashflood had unnerved me, how I had imagined Dr. M.'s face turning into a wolf's face, how I tried to tell the story of Little Red Riding Hood and couldn't remember its end. I wanted a transcript, something like a legal document.

She took what amounted to a dictation and promised to send it to me when she typed it up. I thanked her and took the rest of the day off, shaken by this experience for which I had no name. I would soon turn 55 and celebrate my twentieth wedding anniversary. My older son was going off to college; my younger son was becoming an accomplished musician like Robbie. Trauma, I thought, had an even longer half-life than love.

~ 35 ~

I thought Dr. M. would tell me something about his side of our Little Red Riding Hood session, give me a name for it, or at least his understanding of what had transpired, but after noting calmly that it had been "intense," he turned my question back on me. What had my experience of it been?

I told him how I had dictated what I remembered of the session to a lawyer friend, and how a therapist friend had explained it to me. She said that many of her patients used a fairy tale, or a book, or a movie episode to tell a story they were as yet unable to tell. "They use that scaffolding until they're ready to talk about themselves." I went back to forgetting what else I said in analysis.

I discussed Little Red with Robbie. He had spent decades researching fairy tales and myths. I had often thought that Robbie should be the one lecturing at universities — not me — but, somehow, despite his mind, his research and writing a well-received music textbook, he hadn't been able to pull his extensive investigations together. He continued to dislike institutions and preferred to compose music and to produce recordings of singers and other musicians in his own studio.

That did not stop him from arranging an academic gig for me out west. In the spring of 2003, I was invited by a professor at the university where Kate taught to give a series of workshops on memoir, family history and trauma. Robbie would attend and we would spend a few days together as we had two years before, when I visited him in California.

Patrick was ready to take me to the airport when I received an email from Kate telling me to take a cab to the B & B where I would stay.

That was unusual. I wondered why Robbie himself hadn't called or emailed, but chalked it up to his unpredictability. After I landed, I easily found a taxi and was driven past several motels to an attractive house. Kate was waiting in the cozy living room. Gracious and apologetic, she told me that Robbie had flown to Berlin the previous day.

"It was unexpected," she said, reading the shock on my face. "An unusual business opportunity."

"An unusual business opportunity?" I repeated.

"Lower your voice," Kate whispered, though the B & B was empty. "It's a small town. He's a public person."

Something's secret, I understood.

"Will he be back before I leave?" I asked.

"I can't talk about it," she said and, as soon as the professor who had invited me arrived, disappeared.

Monica and I hit it off at first sight. She swept me into the routines of a visiting author, introduced me to colleagues and students, and offered to translate my memoir into Spanish. She was fascinated by my project with Robbie and sympathetic to my disappointment at finding him gone. But she knew nothing about his sudden trip and Kate had been clear about not wanting to discuss it.

Robbie resurfaced a month later, launching a long, rambling telephone monologue.

"This is your friend Rob," he began, "I have an answer to the waterfall. It was in fact a warning."

It took me a moment to orient myself. He was talking as though I knew what had been passing through his mind or as though a conversation had been interrupted.

"Things like what happened to you at the waterfall happen very often at sacred sites. I've been working on the Indian trails and burial mounds, the Indian Holocaust in the Northwest. I've been in Germany. In touch with rolling back the Nazi Holocaust. Part of a pattern."

I didn't know what to say. Even for Robbie, that was far-fetched.

"Where are you now?" I asked. I was still angry that he had stood me up.

"Back home," he replied. "I was in Berlin for a while. I stayed at the Adlon — where Colin Powell and Bush stay when they're in Berlin. I met a woman who runs a concert series there. And some people who're interested in having me lecture. History of the Ku Klux Klan and history of the Nazis. I'd like to set up a continuum where the Northwest and Berlin are connected. You can feel the murder in both places. You can't get away from it. Fighting racism through pan-culturalism. It's going to be rather big. I'm looking at the same patterns everywhere which, as you know, is what I do..."

I could no longer not recognize what I had refused to know for so long. Grandiosity, finding patterns in everything, spending large amounts of money, disappearing and re-appearing on impulse — all the hallmarks of a manic phase. Robbie had sometimes denied mental illness, or tried to mask it with chronic fatigue. But he had also talked enough about mood disorders that it had been my choice to ignore them.

"My car went off the road a few days ago, but I'm OK."

"That's lucky," I said. Feelings of shock, anger and frustration vied for primacy in my mind. I listened, feeling helpless, and very much alone. Kate would have been the best person for me to talk to but she was covering for Robbie.

Instead, I phoned Robbie's old friend Mike, at whose home we had slept two years before, and asked him whether he knew what was going on. Reluctantly, I thought, Mike told me that he did, and that this was not Robbie's first manic episode. He had been hospitalized before but, after a few weeks, signed himself out of hospital. Typically, Robbie took meds until he decided to stop taking them. We, his friends, had to accept that Robbie had a chronic and dangerous mental illness.

I was relieved to hear confirmation of what I knew. Yet I continued to pretend I didn't know and to treat his illness as a secret. Just as I had slipped notes to my mother under the bathroom door to make sure she was still alive, I wrote short, daily emails to Robbie.

Robbie sent back disconnected fragments of a story: that Kate was letting him stay in their home for the time being; then, that she was no longer allowing him to set foot in the house; then that he was sleeping in the Mercedes he had bought, moving between campsites that had wi-fi. He was thinking about driving down to Texas or flying back to Berlin. He felt good. And he was thinking about "our parallel journeys."

I didn't think our journeys were parallel, I told Dr. M. but I was finally beginning to understand some connections between my relation to Robbie and to my mother.

"Do you think she suffered from manic depression?" Dr. M. asked.

I hadn't thought much about manic depression at all, I said, but suddenly remembered that she had been given that diagnosis back in the early 1960s by the German government. After a decade of suing for reparations for the physical and psychological damage she had sustained as a prisoner in *koncentrák,* she had won her case. I had interviewed her about that long legal process for my first book and found the recording that I had filed away.

In it, my mother explained that soon after the war, Czech Jews were awarded a dollar a day from the time they were forced to wear the Jewish star to the time they were liberated. She had found that payment ridiculous but considered it "more ridiculous" not to accept it in the 1950s when my father was unemployed and every dollar counted. "That first payment," she says on the recording, "disappeared into the bottomless pit of the Epstein household on 67th St."

A decade later, when they were on their feet financially, more substantial reparations were offered and my parents argued about whether or not to apply. Kurt refused but Franci decided to sue.

"An internist gave me a check-up and sent me to various specialists," she says in her most sardonic tone of voice. "All agreed I was a semi-invalid. I had ulcerative colitis and impairment of movement in the left leg and constant backaches. But the Germans never acknowledged the physical damage."

Between sentences, I can hear her light a cigarette, inhale, expel smoke. The doctor who examined her was "a former army officer who introduced himself as a representative of the German government. He was putting me on trial — that was what was so explosive. He gave me the usual neurological exam. Then he asked: why did you go into analysis? Because I was suicidal, I said. Why were you suicidal? Why did you want to kill the children?"

Was that true? On the recording, I don't interrupt my mother. I say nothing and she continues, "Why did I want to kill the children? Because I thought we had no business being here at all. Because I was meant to be dead and have no business being alive. He asked, if you want to be dead, why did you have children? I replied that three children didn't begin to compensate for the number of dead in my family. I started screaming that he had no business asking why I had three children, crying, shaking. He did nothing to calm me down. Then he said: I will send the report to Germany. I left his office shaking. He reported that I was 36% *meshugah, verrückt,* manic depressive."

There it was, in her own voice. I had forgotten that too. Love, loyalty and maybe identification with my mother had required rejecting the psychiatrist and his diagnosis. But, I thought when I searched my memory further, the denial was not one-sided. Sometimes she named or alluded to the disease and sometimes she denied it — just like Robbie. Driving in the countryside, we sometimes passed a state mental hospital. My mother would look out at the barred windows and declare, unasked, that she would never, ever, consent to be confined there.

Mental illness is still a stigma in many cultures. As long as I could remember, my mother had conflated or camouflaged her psychological issues with physical ones — migraines, back, leg and stomach pains — in the same way Robbie camouflaged his bipolar disease with chronic fatigue syndrome. I had colluded in guarding their secret.

Hearing my mother's tape and having a transcript of my Little Red Riding Hood session to reread and annotate made me realize the importance of testimony and witness emphasized in Judith Herman's trauma seminar. I was aware that recording therapy sessions was the privilege of teaching professionals rather than patients, but I thought it would help me to record and listen to my own. It was always a qualitatively different experience for me to read my books after I wrote them. I could take in the import of my words, grasp their significance. But I thought that my by-the-book analyst would refuse to entertain the idea of my recording myself; he certainly would insist on examining what it meant.

Sure enough he asked, "What are your thoughts?"

I didn't want to offend him by pointing out that while he did a good job tracking my associations, he had a network of his own associations that could get in the way. In a rare breach of technique, for example, he had once confessed that my dead grandmother Pepi's name reminded him of a Brazilian soccer player!

So I fell back on my own professional norms: I told him that in reporting, recording an interview was routine for accuracy. Exact wording and tone of voice were important to characterize an interviewee. In addition, I had often reaped a huge benefit by re-engaging with the material when I transcribed recordings, read and re-read them, annotating themes and important points. I ran phrases through my body until I was satisfied that I understood the multiplicity of meanings contained in them.

The only person who had ever challenged my practice of using a tape recorder was a paranoid university president who had insisted on taping our interviews himself and having his secretary type the transcript. A control freak, but a smart one, I had thought at the time: protecting himself, amassing material he might later use, preserving his own record, maybe leveling the playing field after his experiences of being misquoted and/or misunderstood.

My personal reasons for wanting to record myself were that, despite my understanding of dissociation and episodic amnesia, I was still not remembering much of what I said in session and that disturbed me. Though I had begun my memoir with the idea of relying on Robbie's memory, I now wanted to rely on my own — not Dr. Mr.'s. In the psychiatric literature it was always the doctor who wrote up the case. I could read Freud's narrative of his work with Dora but not her version.

"As I understand it, you're going to tape only yourself," Dr. M. said.

"Yes, but that's unusual, isn't it?" I recalled the technical terms from Dr. Herman's seminar. "It modifies the therapeutic frame, it could be interpreted as trangressive and/or as a defense."

I paused but all he said was, "Go on."

I thought about tape recorders. Robbie had used one for his broadcasts. Ivan had used one for his, long before I became a journalist. A tape recorder was a tool of my trade. Weapon, fall-back, protection. Damn free association, I thought. Also agency, control, invasion of privacy, truth, propaganda and missiles in the Cold War.

"I want to hear my own voice," I told Dr. M., refusing to think about issues of power.

"Your voice?" I thought I heard sarcasm in his. "You have a strong voice. Do you think I don't hear you?"

"The point is I don't always hear myself. What good is having a strong voice if I can't hear it?"

To my surprise, my analyst agreed to my use of a tape recorder on my end of our phone sessions. In November of 2003, I began taping them.

~ 36 ~

The recordings made for unexpectedly boring listening, so boring that I felt sorry for Dr. M. My journalistic recordings were usually lucid and entertaining. My interviewees told anecdotes that explained how their lives and relationships had evolved. I stumbled, chattered, paused. And since I only recorded my end of sessions, there were many dead spots.

But the recordings were infinitely interesting to me and very useful in reflecting on my tone of voice, my selection of words or story. I could press "Stop," as I could not in ordinary conversation or even in session, and replay my words as many times as necessary to understand what I had said or meant, separate wheat from chaff, trace the narrative line.

When I traveled to Manhattan for a face-to-face session, however, I felt obliged to leave my tape recorder at home. Though I had become accustomed to recording my end of sessions and would have liked to record my analyst and our interaction too, I didn't want to push my luck.

I was accustomed, after nearly three years of visiting him in his office, to feeling uneasy in the small lobby and elevator. This time, as the door opened, I froze. I saw Dr. M. wearing a black leather jacket engaged in conversation with another tall man, blocking my way into the corridor.

They stopped talking and moved aside. Dr. M. hurried to his suite and I followed, disturbed but striving for nonchalance. Black leather was in fashion that winter and my analyst liked to dress fashionably. But I thought: hood, juvenile delinquent, gangster, Nazi — a conflation of my parents' and my own symbols of male power.

As Dr. M. closed his office door behind us, I noticed myself checking out his bookshelves and desk and the way he settled back into his Eames chair. I sat down in my usual chair facing him and a large window shaded with white Venetian blinds. All seemed to be going according to our usual pattern and I was in the middle of a sentence when Dr. M. suddenly got up, turned, and adjusted the blinds.

Inside me, something froze and my brain went into overdrive: had I been squinting? Was the reflection of my glasses making it hard for him to see the expression in my eyes. Why shouldn't he have adjusted the blinds? Why was this an issue? I decided to ignore it and forgot everything I said after that moment. But by the time I returned to Massachusetts, I realized that I had been scared, pretended I wasn't, and said nothing. If I couldn't tell Dr. M. about that, what was I doing in analysis?

In our next session, at home, I pressed "Record" and told Dr. M. I wanted to analyze what had happened to me in his office, and listen to what I said. That's what we did and, again I couldn't remember most of what I said.

But this time, I could hear it. I heard my voice rise in pitch, until it sounded like a peevish child's voice. "In our session last time, I remember asking you why you got up to change the blinds and then... Oh God (a whisper) I can't remember anything."

My voice breaks, then stops.

"I can't remember the sequence and I can't remember... well, I guess instead of trying to remember, I should just say whatever comes to mind, right?"

Dr. M. must have said yes, because my voice grows stronger and steadier. "In Massachusetts," I declare, "when you visit your doctor, he tells you what he's going to do before he does it. So it was very unexpected when you got up and closed the blinds. That was number one. Number two, it didn't make sense to me.

Because the light was coming in behind you, so I couldn't understand why you were doing what you were doing."

Listening to my voice on the tape recorder, I can hear my indignation as well as my confusion about his action, my fear of learning something I don't want to know, my fear that he'll say what bothers me is childish and not worth talking about.

"I wanted to ask you right away why you adjusted the blinds but didn't. And when I finally did, you didn't answer. Is that accurate? Am I remembering this right?"

Dr. M. must have said yes, because I continue. We had had a long, frustrating discussion about whether the lighting in his office was dim or bright. Eventually, Dr. M. had said, "this discussion of light isn't interesting."

In that moment, I had agreed with him. I didn't understand why or how we had gotten into a discussion of light. But as I listened to the recording I realized what I hadn't been able to say: that black leather jackets scared me, and that it had been even more scary when he suddenly got up to close the blinds. Maybe there had been window blinds at Ivan's house. Certainly the man in the Schwab House had opened his window blinds so Judy and I could watch him masturbate.

Only after I had listened to my recording of that session several times did I give Dr. M. a piece of my mind. How could he suddenly get up in session without warning? Why hadn't he understood that it would bother me? How could he say my fuss about the blinds was not interesting? I thought: my father said that! and the realization plunged me into despair. Had I complained to my father about Ivan and not made myself clear? Had he misunderstood or dismissed my complaint as unimportant? I expected him to be able connect the dots and was furious that he had not.

"It's lousy technique to say something isn't interesting to a patient. If you want someone to talk, you have to make them feel like everything they say is interesting."

Dr. M. suggested that I felt demeaned by his comment.

"Not demeaned," I clarified, feeling as though I were challenging him for the first time. "It was dismissive of the importance of what I was telling you."

It would be satisfying to say that after this episode, I became steadily more forthcoming and uncensored. But I was more like a toddler learning how to walk. Two steps forward. A fall. Trying again. A misunderstanding or unpleasant exchange took days to untangle and made me doubt my trust in the process yet again. I was still forgetting what I said in session but listening to the recording enabled me to hear what it was I wanted to say.

~ 37 ~

I continued to keep the content of my analysis quarantined from my husband and sons. They knew I was writing a book, but didn't ask what it was about. Patrick always preferred to read only the final drafts of my writing and I had come to appreciate the freedom this allowed me. By January of 2004, we had been living in our New England town for five years and Patrick was the famous person in our family, a controversial figure in local politics. I liked the anonymity of being known only as his wife in a culture where few people asked personal questions.

I was deeply absorbed in my writing and psychoanalysis.

Sometimes as I mailed my monthly check to Dr. M. I felt incensed at the unfairness of having to spend my time and money on the fall-out of other people's behavior. But I had stopped weeping, stopped feeling the choking sensations in my throat, and felt sure that dismantling years of self-protective habits required a slow, careful process. I saw my psychoanalysis as a second chance at childhood, this time with a (mostly) empathic and available parent.

Winter is usually gloomy in New England but I found it particularly bleak that year. My father's birthday was at the end of January, and his date of death February 1. I found myself reflecting on our relationship.

Kurt had wanted his first-born to be a daughter and named me Helena after his adored, murdered mother. Since he was unemployed for much of my childhood, he was the parent who taught me how to swim and ice skate and ride a bike. Often we delivered packages to my mother's customers together or went on errands to pick up items from her many suppliers. I had served as my father's translator, helper and guide to the city.

Dr. M. more than once observed that I sometimes treated him as though he needed help too. "Since you're stuck with me, you might as well educate me," he once said after I had recommended that he read yet another book.

I chose not to bring up Dr. Herman's book, but agreed. I told Dr. M. that when we lived in our first tiny apartment and my mother had customer fittings in the living room, my father and I rode the Staten Island Ferry all day. We shuttled back and forth across New York Harbor, throwing breadcrumbs to the seagulls, getting off and back on the ferry every 30 minutes. We had lunch at the food counter and he ordered hot dogs with sauerkraut on the white rolls we never ate at home. Kurt would say, *"To je ale bašta,"* or "What a feast!" One time, he discovered he didn't have any money to pay.

"What happened?" Dr. M. asked.

A nice American lady noticed and paid.

Dr. M. asked. "Were you embarrassed?"

"I don't think so," I said. I have fond memories of the ferry and of hot dogs with sauerkraut. But Dr. M.'s question focused my attention on idealizing my father, unlike my brother who called him "a fish out of water in America." In my mother's account, Kurt was the healthy survivor. But was he so healthy? Although he was never suicidal and an optimist, he had his rages and absent-minded, possibly depressive moods. He expected me to be happy and active, not pensive. When I looked anything but busy, he would declaim a Czech poem of reproach *Zas v okně zadumán* so often that I knew it by heart. "Once again at the window? Yearning for far away? Where are your thoughts roving, where?"

I wondered where my father's thoughts had been while Ivan was defiling his home. Had he not noticed what was going on?

But I didn't, at first, say that to Dr. M. It would have been disloyal.

Though I felt a wordless sympathy with my father, my mother repeatedly asserted her claim on my loyalty early on, just as her mother had claimed hers. She saw us as allies, our alliance sealed by our physical resemblance. Unlike my father, who shared with me his comfort in the physical, my mother shared cultural life: books, theater and music. I was, early on, her chosen intellectual partner and emotional confidante.

Franci often invited me into the bathroom for an evening chat. I sat on the edge of the tub while she soaked in the steaming water. She had gone without hot water during the war and indulged every evening while I entertained her with stories from school. I was both accustomed to and disturbed by the sight of my mother's body, especially her breasts like empty sacks against her ribs. I thought they, like her Auschwitz tattoo, were a consequence of the war, but Franci said no. In that inimitable tone of voice, she said that she had breast-fed all three of us children, and we had sucked her dry.

That winter, I dreamed of bathtubs, swimming pools, floating, diving or drowning in water. In one dream I drew for Dr. M., he and I had exchanged places in his office. I was sitting in his chair and he was lying on the couch, both of us oblivious to the water rising from the floor. In another, I was a toddler in a bathtub. The water was running; I could hear the sound. My mother and Ivan were in the bathroom and the door was locked. My father was elsewhere in the apartment. The scene looked like an illustration from the Czech children's books that Ivan had framed for my brothers and me.

Water was such a multifaceted symbol — of life, sensuality, relaxation, play, danger, and death. It was in our bathtub that I chose to stand with my roommate when we were mugged in our home, but I had once given Robbie a bath in that tub when he appeared, tired and disheveled, at my door. Was the tub where Ivan and my mother had sex together? Or was I in the tub and they next to it, when they stole time together with the excuse of giving me a bath? Had they made love and lost consciousness of me sitting in the rising water? How could I remember?

Though I knew he wouldn't answer, I asked Dr. M., "Do you believe nothing happened with Ivan?"

"I'm where you are on this," he replied. "*Something* happened. I don't yet know exactly what."

Each time he refused to speculate, I was reminded of the False Memory Syndrome establishment who, for decades, blamed therapists with their own agendas for leading patients into false accusations of sexual abuse and consigning innocent people to prison. The presumption of innocence until proven guilty was deeply ingrained in me; I had learned it in grammar school and it had resonated even more strongly because my parents and their friends had been innocent people in prison. Ivan, too, had been one of those prisoners, a political hero.

That spring of 2004, my friend whose therapeutic relationship had turned into a sexual one finally ended her therapy and checked into a residential treatment center. I visited her there. Over tea in the sitting room, my friend told me that she was beginning to understand her sexual involvement as abuse rather than "affair." She had a woman therapist at the center and had become aware of the extent of her dissociative capacities. During her last session, for example, she had been so caught up in what she was saying that she hadn't noticed her ankle had been braced against the heater and later discovered that she had a severe burn on her shin. I left feeling worried for her and angry.

Driving home, my mind once again filled with images of a bathroom and a bathtub: faucets on the wall above a spout; a white tub; a lock on the door. These images weren't a fantasy or hypothetical, I thought. Alone, in my office after dinner, while Patrick was at yet another Town Meeting, I took out my sketchbook, determined to draw the bathtub of my dream with its faucets and spout.

But something odd happened. The faucets I wanted to sketch morphed in my mind into testicles and I put my pencil down, stopped drawing, put away the sketchbook.

The next day I screwed up my courage and told Dr. M. the sequence of events. But instead of waiting patiently as he usually did, Dr. M. started speaking so rapidly that I could barely take it in — about nudity in our household: my parents' exhibitionism, the overstimulation of a young child. Though he didn't say it explicitly, I had the sense that he found my family's way of life outrageous.

"I don't understand why you're so certain about this," I heard myself say when I played back the recording. "It's not just my parents who walked around naked or in their underwear — it's a Czech thing. It was normal to me."

Dr. M. must have argued that I was making his point: that my family had normalized behavior that was not normative. No child could integrate the nakedness of adults. It surpassed all limits; why else would it be so much on my mind?

"It wasn't on my mind until I started writing this damn book," I say. "My father's cold showers and walking out of the bathroom in his terrycloth loincloth was a joke: his idea of an American Indian. My father's not important here. What's important is that something else happened in that bathroom. It happened again when I tried to draw it."

I think — I can't say for sure because I was not recording his side of our session — that Dr. M. reminded me that my father had taken me swimming with him when I was a child, to a pool in Brooklyn, and taken me into the locker room with him. Wasn't it likely we had showered together?

Probably, I thought, though I had no memories of it. My memories of going swimming with my father were happy ones, like those on the Staten Island Ferry. We took the subway to the immensely long St. George swimming pool in Brooklyn. Sometimes he had a massage there. I don't know where I was during that time. But after a few hours there we went to a luncheonette and ate at the counter. I remembered eating a delicious rice pudding.

Yes, I probably saw naked men in the locker room and my father naked in the shower. But so what? He wasn't scary. Ivan was scary.

I felt as though Dr. M. was devising a benevolent interpretation of what I told him. He had lifted me out of that tub to a safer place — a shower — where I could not drown. He meant well and I wished that had been the case but Dr. M. was wrong. Once again, I questioned his competence. Then I remembered his family's background. Maybe he was simply unable to imagine a Jewish family so unlike his own.

Listening to the recording, I can hear in my voice when I decided to assert myself. "I'd like to understand why when I started drawing faucets in a bathtub, they turned into testicles. It has nothing to do with a shower or my father. It has to do with my mother and Ivan and the door was locked and they were doing something together — and they forgot about me and maybe I nearly drowned in that tub. That may be a total fantasy. I may have made the whole thing up, but even saying it makes me feel like I'm slipping and falling."

"You're defending your father," I remember — though I cannot prove — that he said.

"How am I defending my father?" I argue though I know I'm defending my father. Why would I criticize him? He was my sane parent, the one I didn't feel I had to work to keep alive.

Yet since this was psychoanalysis — not ordinary conversation — I tried to remember something that really bothered me about my late father. What came to mind was a soiled washcloth left carelessly on the bathroom sink that not only my whole family, but my mother's customers and employees used. Kurt, who had grown up in the Czech countryside without toilet paper sometimes used a washcloth to finish wiping himself, forgot to wash it out, and left it lying there.

That galvanized Dr. M. He reacted with a kind of prolonged yelp. *"EEEyuuuww!"* Then, casting neutrality to the winds, he unleashed a torrent of words in which I caught only "No culture in the world..." that ended only when he realized we had gone well past our 50 minutes. Only then did he collect himself and say, "You'll be glad to know it's time to stop."

I was both glad and furious at my analyst. What the hell was he doing? Was his yelp some kind of analytic ploy? Or was he really unnerved? Modeling for me his idea of how I as a child would have been disgusted? Or had my memory touched on some toilet training preoccupation he had? Was he frustrated that I wasn't progressing? Sorry that he had taken me on as a scholarship analysand? I was even more sorry. He probably preferred psychopharm to analysis, prescribing meds at $400 each 20 minutes.

He had taken control of our session, forced an interpretation down my throat, pressed me to be critical of my father. I had complied by producing an episode critical of my father and then Dr. M. had gone berserk, going on about how outrageous it was that Kurt wiped his ass with a washcloth and left it on the sink.

He didn't have to convince me. It had disturbed me enough to remember it decades later. That was why I had told him about it. But how could I trust him with my family if he was so judgmental? It made me worry what else he had judged disgusting all the times he was silent. Did he think any of our parents had Charmin toilet tissue during the war? Was this, given the context, the most important thing to be shocked about?

"You've never so much as said 'That's too bad' when I talked about my mother threatening to kill herself," I wrote to him in an email. *"Or hitting me, or telling me that her kids 'sucked her dry' or having an affair with Ivan. How can you make a fuss about a dirty washcloth? He should have remembered to wash it out. He should have put it under the sink. He didn't. But I'm not haunted by it. I don't have dreams about dirty washcloths."*

Next session, Dr. M. apologized for being a bull in a china shop. Though he didn't explain what, exactly, he meant, I was pleased. I rarely heard apologies — not from my parents when they were alive, not from Patrick or my sons, not from Robbie. I was also somewhat pleased with myself for having "talked back" to Dr. M. and apparently not offended him. He's a good enough shrink, I told myself. I'm changing, learning; we repair and go on. It's like marriage.

My marriage seemed to be doing well as I maintained my policy of strict quarantine. A couple of my friends kept worrying that my book and my analysis were taking a toll on Patrick. I didn't think so but I asked him whether that was the case.

My husband looked blank, then said, "It would be difficult for me if you were preoccupied with shopping for clothes. It's good that you're absorbed in your therapy. It's good you have Robbie to help you with your book."

~ 38 ~

For the next several months, Robbie was homeless, moving between motels, campsites and trailer parks. But my long idolization of him seemed impervious to his mental breakdown or change in circumstance. The sound of his voice continued to ground me. Friends thought it crazy that I would draw stability from such an unstable person, but for reasons that remained mysterious, I did. The internet made it possible for us to remain in steady contact, and Robbie suggested that now that he was on his own, he had more time for long emails and phone conversations with me. He said that he found true revolution in the itinerant life and was learning much about America from his fellow travelers.

I listened to him with a mix of incredulity and sorrow, and wondered who else was tethering him to his past, hearing his reports from the margins of American life. Robbie kept his various friends separate. I knew he had had dozens, including many women, but that he had also burned dozens of bridges. I was among the loyalists. For the last four years he had been a lifesaver for me. I wanted to be the same for him.

I ignored my dismay about his living in trailer parks and emailing from down and out towns along back roads as he made his way across the continent. He talked to me about his state of mind and marriage; I talked about the progress of my analysis, and my still crippling and recurrent bouts of doubt, about Ivan's molestation of me. Unlike Dr. M., Robbie rarely passed up an opportunity to voice his opinion. "Why would you make this stuff up?" he asked. "You're not the type that makes things up. You're too literal."

He emailed from a trailer park with wi-fi: *"You've always been attracted to people in trouble. We're all stand-ins for what you would have felt for yourself had you been allowed to feel anything. You start out writing about a teenage infatuation. But I'm only the sideshow: important but not the real stuff. You discover that your mother was involved with a man who was supposed to be taking care of you. She not only disallowed feelings, she ridiculed your physical and sexual sense of self while — incredibly — allowing a man she was involved with to molest you."*

He was, I remembered, the son of a screenwriter, accustomed since childhood to discussions of character and script. He was so perceptive. How could he be mentally ill?

Patrick was shocked by what I told him of Robbie's situation and wondered aloud whether we should offer to house him in our basement. Not a good idea, I told my husband. Better to stay in regular contact, hope he worked things out with his wife, and support him from a distance.

During our telephone chats, I tried to listen to Robbie in the way Dr. M. at his best listened to me: dispassionately, trying to remain calm while following and sorting through what I said. Robbie insisted that he had never been manic. Bad diagnosis. Those changed every few years anyway, and it was hard to find a good psychiatrist. He was sure his breakdown was the consequence of misguided doctors prescribing Valium and Prozac. His complicated family history and experiences in Mississippi had caused PTSD. He was better off meds, had lost weight.

Now that he was living alone, he had made up his mind to focus on writing his own family history. The whole thing, including his mother's background, his father's background, the blacklist. He was grappling with what I had described in those *études* I had written, especially about privacy. Once again, he referred to our "parallel journeys" as writers. He was tired of trying to protect people. We should both name real names in our books, he said. He would use mine; I should use his.

I didn't entirely buy into his idea of parallel journeys. Yes, we were both ex-New Yorkers in our fifties with a history of trauma, looking back over our lives. But that was where the similarity ended. Robbie wasn't a writer; he was a musician and a political activist. I was neither. Naming names was still a highly-charged issue in his left-wing community fifty years after the blacklisting of American Communists and not a good idea for me either. My experience as a reporter was that many stable people denied everything they said for the record, and some sued after they saw their words in print. Robbie was a litigious man who had once sued his local police force. It was impossible to predict what would upset him. I had once described an advertising executive as "sturdily-built" in a magazine article; she had threatened to withdraw advertising unless the publisher removed the adjective.

Describing people was a minor infraction compared to divulging their secrets. Robbie and I had both grown up with the necessity of keeping secrets. Now we were both writing about them. In that, I conceded, we were alike.

I brought that issue of complicity in secrets to Dr. M. who, since he never confided in me, never burdened me with any secrets. It seemed to me that secrets had burdened me for as long I could remember. Listening, being loyal, keeping secrets, had seemed to me an indispensable part of love. Now I felt privy to too many secrets: secrets about extra-marital love affairs, abortions, drug addiction, alcoholism, mental health, prior marriages. I no longer regarded secrets as fun, or solely as expressions of trust and camaraderie; I became aware of keeping secrets as a burden.

Suddenly, I thought I understood the underlying reason why I had quit working with my woman analyst, Dr. M.'s predecessor, 30 years earlier. Every Friday, I told Dr. M., I recognized the man sitting in her waiting room as the editor of the *New Yorker.* I had met him as a grad student, interviewing for a job at his magazine. He had asked me why I wanted to check facts. I had burst into tears and said that I actually didn't. He had handed me a box of tissues and taken half an hour out of his busy schedule to talk to me.

He sat, head leaned against his hand, looking down as I grabbed my coat and left. I had read and heard about his famous need for privacy and didn't mention my weekly sighting of him to anyone. But Dr. Young startled me one Friday morning by not waiting for me to free-associate, but asking: did I recognize the man in the waiting room?

When I said I did, she looked alarmed and instructed me to keep my observation to myself. I was new to analysis then, hyper-obedient, unaware of the many ramifications of that instruction. I was also a young writer, thrilled to be sharing an analyst with the venerated editor of the *New Yorker.* She was an analytic elder, seeing me at a vastly reduced rate. Looking back on it, I think Dr. Young was — consciously or unconsciously — subsuming my interests to interests of her wealthier and much more prestigious analysand: an older man with whom she shared a deep relationship. Though I made no protest at being asked to keep a secret then — though I felt excited, even honored by her appeal to my loyalty — some part of me must have resented being low in a hierarchy of patients, and being told to keep a secret in someone else's interest.

Dr. M. made no comment — Dr. Young had referred me to him, and I assumed he had loyalty issues of his own. Maybe she had been his teacher or supervisor. I told him I was glad he had never asked me anything like that, and I thought he seemed to make an even greater effort to see things from my point of view. I complained that, after a year of recording only my end of our sessions, it was hard to reconstruct his end. I told him that technology allowed journalists to hook their phones up to their computers for interviews, and asked if I might do that for our sessions.

He agreed and I took his agreement to be a further deepening of the trust between us. A few months later when I came into the city, I brought my tape recorder to his office. It felt a little strange to press "Record" but even stranger when his answering machine went on and a patient identified herself before Dr. M. figured out how to switch the mechanism off. I recognized the caller's voice and name as those of a classmate at Hunter High School and told him so. Dr. M. remained poker faced and silent. I wondered whether he was embarrassed at being technologically challenged — he had once described himself as a Luddite — or whether he was trying to encourage me to speak my mind. But I said nothing beyond telling him that the caller had sat behind me in Latin class. I didn't point out that he had made a choice different from his mentor's. Something very ingrained in me resisted even talking about the theme of secrecy.

I had less trouble addressing collective secrets. In the spring of 2005, my Hunter High School classmates were preparing a 40th reunion and exchanging news and questions on our listserv. I seized upon the opportunity to raise a question I had never raised while we were teenagers: was anyone still thinking about the unpleasant, often disgusting sexual encounters — I did not yet formulate them as assaults — with men that we experienced traveling to and from school on public transportation?

The response was an example of what Dr. Herman had cited as the power of cultural and collective validation. *"I saw far too many penises on the way to school from Queens,"* wrote one classmate. *"Had hands up my skirt, strap-hangers masturbate right in my face with their hand in their pants. I was extremely disturbed but felt helpless to do anything but try to move away, not easy in a crowded train. I never asked for help, nor did I feel I ever would have gotten any. Now this is finally becoming public. Why did it take so long?"*

"It was midday," wrote another classmate, *"and I was heading for the subway exit when a man pushed in front of me — I never saw his face — and placed his hand in my crotch. I was appalled and ashamed. Nothing like this had ever happened to me before. I tried to tell my mother and she dismissed it as if it*

weren't important or had somehow been my fault. That made me feel injured all over again."

Some of my classmates hadn't told their parents because they thought it wouldn't change anything; some were afraid that if they complained, their parents might transfer them to another school. One remembered the example of a plucky girl with whom she often took the subway, *"I was always too terrified to do anything, but Frenchy grabbed a man's hand as he was inching it up under her skirt, held it in the air and yelled out, 'Who belongs to this hand?' I never would have had the guts to do it."*

Very few of us had responded in this way although some lucky girls — the ones who barely remembered or made light of these episodes — had received practical instructions from their mothers and grandmothers. A British friend whom I told this to remembered her mother's instruction to jump to her feet if a man bothered her on the bus, and say, as loudly as possible, "You must stop that!" Her mother had practiced saying it with her and the next time a man started groping her on the bus, she spoke up loud and clear.

Her mother was a teacher, unusually attuned to the needs of children. My mother and many of my classmates' mothers, apparently, were not. No one mentioned that fathers might have had something to say about the issue.

After smart phones came into general use, I was thrilled to read a newspaper article about a quick-witted girl on the subway who had turned the tables on an exhibitionist. Using her phone, she snapped a series of penis photos and the face of the man it belonged to. She showed them to her principal, who called the police. The photos were published in New York City's largest newspaper. The perp was arrested.

Here was a girl much like I had been, a daughter of new immigrants unwilling to burden her parents with her problems, who had instead mobilized her brain, new technology and cultural change to her advantage. She sought help from an enlightened principal who listened to her and acted on her behalf.

I was elated by this newspaper article. I shared it with friends and speculated that a new telephone that took pictures could become the way to end sexual harassment. But, as I wrote my analyst his monthly check, I again felt a swell of irritation at having to pay to repair an injury another man had inflicted long ago. I recognized it as the ember of a rage I felt against all the men who were still getting away with far worse, all over the world.

I had been carrying that unexpressed rage around for most of my life. Now, when it was triggered by some small injustice, it welled up without warning, outsize, paralyzing me. My rage at Ivan had been mixed up with my rage at the Nazis, men who towered above all other criminals in my mind. I knew that, of course, there had been female Nazis too, but I thought of the murderers as men. I realized that for most of my life I had mistrusted almost any man — teacher, editor, colleague — who held power. That kind of man was inherently suspect and corrupt — like the Roman Emperor Caligula to whom I had associated the first time I saw Dr. M. in person.

The men I admired or had fallen in love with were, I thought in retrospect, challengers to power, anti-establishment, counter-culture teenagers like Robbie or victims of power, like my immigrant father. That avoidance of powerful, successful men had complicated my romantic life and made it difficult to choose a life partner. It was hard to find a man who met my peculiar criterion and, given my history with my mother, impossible to trust a woman.

~ 39 ~

What had my mother known and not known about Ivan's treatment of me? Had I complained to her? Had she employed her formidable powers of denial and dissociation? Gotten angry? Hit me?

I told Dr. M. about a long-ago book fair luncheon in Atlanta where a well-dressed woman stood up during the Q and A and declared, in a Czech accent, that I looked just like my mother. The elegant stranger had been in a work camp with Franci in northern Germany toward the end of the war. It was winter and freezing cold. The Allies were bombing. A few girls began crying. Franci had scolded them: "How could they give the Germans such satisfaction? They were Czechs! They were Jews! She had demanded that they sing."

My face froze while my heart took a dive. I knew this story. My mother's cousin in Prague was also a prisoner in that German work camp. So were other survivors whom I had interviewed. They all repeated the fantastic tale of my mother, who had had the presence of mind and audacity to lie to Dr. Mengele during a selection for life or extermination at Auschwitz by claiming she was an electrician instead of a dressmaker. Though it had not helped her in Auschwitz, when their group was transported to a work camp in the last cold months of the war, Franci was in the files as an electrician.

It was a dangerous position since, although her father had been an electrical engineer, Franci knew next to nothing about the job of electrician. She had lied her way to that designation, never thinking that she would be called upon to actually work with live wires. But she learned on the job and reaped the rewards of what prisoners who worked outside in the brickyard regarded as cushy indoor work. For a short time, our Prague cousin had told me, Franci had been made a *kapo* by the camp commander. I had reacted by ignoring that scary word.

"One girl was unable to stop sobbing," the elegant stranger was continuing her comment at the Atlanta Book Fair. "Franci slapped her and the girl stopped crying. That was the kind of woman she was."

At the podium, I wondered what, exactly, my questioner meant. Had my mother behaved like a sadist in this woman's eyes? Or as a cheerleader, trying to safeguard the morale of the group? Had her cousin used the word *kapo* loosely to mean "boss"? Or had she meant that my mother had served as a surrogate for the Nazis? My mother was authoritarian and directive. Was that why I was so sensitive to being called bossy?

These thoughts overwhelmed me and I forced them out of consciousness as I acknowledged a series of other women who wished to speak. Their public questions displaced my private, secret ones. The Q and A was followed by a book signing during which no one asked about the slap. I never saw the stranger again but remained troubled by her story.

A couple of years later, at a talk in New York, I heard a strikingly similar one from another woman who had been in that same work camp. Perhaps the two women were describing the same incident but the second survivor's memory was of my mother slapping her in Auschwitz. Their group had been kneeling for hours during an inspection and Lily, who was one of the youngest prisoners, was crying. Franci, Lily told me, had given her a *"facka."* That, I well knew, was the Czech word for slap. Even my non-Czech-speaking brothers knew it.

"Your mother was violent," Dr. M. startled me by saying.

Such a categorical statement from him was rare. It relieved me of the burden of judgment and brought the word *kapo* back to my awareness. I thought: if these women were witnesses to her violence, then it was no secret. My loyalty to her was useless. I told my analyst none of these thoughts.

"Did your father ever slap you?" Dr. M. asked, after a long pause.

"Yes." I said, without hesitation. My father slapped both my brothers and me. But his slaps were predictable and came after several warnings to behave. I could remember arguing with my father over what I perceived to be unjust slaps, blaming him for unfairness. I never felt able to argue with my mother. Her losing control of herself and slapping us was sudden and unpredictable. She had admitted it herself — I had quoted her verbatim in my first book — yet I could not for the life of me remember what she said.

"She gave you permission to remember," Dr. M. noted.

"Yes," I agreed.

"But you resist believing it," Dr. M. said.

"I guess."

I located a copy of *Children of the Holocaust* and read from the book I myself had written, *"You were too little to understand what it was like. Daddy couldn't find a place for himself. He had jobs where every Friday he could be told he would be laid off. Sometimes for three days. Sometimes for two months. The insecurity drove me crazy and I couldn't say anything. I couldn't reproach him because I knew he was doing what he could...*

"I got these terrible broodings. I thought that we were always going to be in this awful pinch when the first of the month came and all those bills had to be paid. You and Tommy weren't the calmest of children. You needed attention. I was working and cooking and cleaning the house and I began to think it all wasn't worth it. I felt trapped. I wanted to kill myself. I wanted to kill you and Tommy too. That's what finally sent me to Dr. Rabinowitz. I was slapping the two of you and it was like I was slapping myself. You don't remember in the morning I would go to the doctor before I started working? Don't you remember?"

I didn't remember when I read her words in my book, and I didn't remember after listening to her voice on a recording. Somehow I had managed to select those sentences for quotation, copied them, placed them in a narrative, and then banished them from consciousness. Even now, my mind kept trying to repeat the psychic trick that resembled the action of a Magic Slate: registering, then erasing, over and over again.

Working through the details with Dr. M. was challenging in many ways and on many levels. I felt like a tattletale telling Dr. M. about her failings. Telling tales was not only disloyal but making mountains out of molehills. I was myself a mother now: God only knew what my sons would complain of about my parenting! She did the best she could. Of course she lost it at times.

But then I did the calculations: my brother Tommy had been born when I was three and half. She wouldn't have beaten up a baby, would she? Tommy must have been walking before she hit him, so I must have been at least five or six. Old enough to remember but I had no memory of being hit by my mother when I was a child. The only time I could remember clearly was when I was 30, and refused her present of aluminum folding chairs for my cottage. When I said I didn't want them, she raised her hand to slap me and my boyfriend had intervened.

I went back over that incident with Dr. M. My boyfriend and my mother had disliked each other. He was a tall, quiet writer, astonished by the intense, dramatic scene that he had witnessed. He wanted to understand what happened and why.

I had no such witness or discussion as a child. My younger brother was younger and slow in acquiring verbal skills. My father usually tuned out my mother's depressions and bouts of violence. Any conversation there was, was conducted in Czech. There had been no outsider like my Midwestern boyfriend to note that what was going on in our house was not normal — until Robbie started coming for dinner.

Unfortunately, I thought, Robbie had missed meeting Ivan. Milena had died soon after I met Robbie. Ivan had moved to

California and died a year later. No one inside the refugee community thought Ivan's habit of chasing me into corners, kissing me on the mouth with his whiskey-wet lips, or taking hundreds of photographs of me unusual. Those things were considered acceptable by the adults in my parents' circle. There was no outsider to question their conventions or that my parents left me alone with my self-styled grandfather.

By my fifth year of therapy, Dr. M.'s silent but perceptible skepticism about my parents and their culture began to pierce through my knee-jerk loyalty to the people I loved most. I began to question that loyalty. In our family the war had trumped and excused everything. But Dr. M., I now knew, had parents who had been in that war as well and he didn't seem to think that the war gave survivors a blank check for behavior.

He sometimes pointed out, calmly, that I had grown up among many troubled adults who had lived through damaging experiences. Their stories and behavior, I began to realize, had conditioned my expectations of people and life. I myself was drawn toward troubled people. I befriended them, took care of them, made few demands of my own. Of course, many of my friends were artists and writers, troubled for reasons that had nothing to do with genocide.

They were injured in other ways. Those injuries seemed to attract me to them. It was as if I applied the template of my relationship with my mother to my friends and kept re-enacting my role of listener and cheerleader, warding off their sadness. I began to notice the pattern when I met new people and noticed, too, that the old attraction was paling.

After five years of observing myself self-censor and withhold information from my doctor, I understood that the after-effects of childhood abuse, for me, extended far beyond seeing phallic symbols in vegetables and water faucets — or even being enraged at predatory men. In fact, the strictly sexual consequences of abuse were minor compared to the way abuse (and its lack of acknowledgement) affected my sense of reality: the very way I trusted my perceptions. Those after-effects interfered in my relationships with other people, affected the way I talked to my analyst, and had created that trio of secrecy, silence and shame in a girl whose bent was the opposite of all three.

I was aware of continuing to operate under cover as I researched and wrote my book, relishing the invisibility I had craved as a child, keeping my objectives to myself as I tried to gather evidence, however circumstantial, about the principal players in my childhood drama.

Though my relationship with him had often been difficult, I called on my mother's only living cousin, a man my brothers and I called "Uncle Peter" though he was not our uncle. He and Franci were first cousins, about the same age, friends since childhood. As teenagers, my mother had told me, they were caught necking in a Prague hotel by Peter's father, whose reprimand had been only that, as first cousins, they could not have sexual relations or marry. I had accepted that story, as so many others from my mother, without question, as I had come to accept their up and down, convoluted relationship, which my mother sometimes seemed to see as a thwarted love affair.

Uncle Peter was as complicated as Franci. He had been able, as a student, to get out of Europe before the war, but his parents and younger brother had been murdered. My mother believed that Peter was burdened by enormous guilt. That was why he had paid for my mother's psychoanalysis, bought the Epsteins their first car, had repeatedly come to the financial rescue when my mother's business was ailing.

Uncle Peter's first and second wives both — understandably, I thought now — resented this diversion of income as well as his intimacy with my mother. I thought, even as a child, that Uncle Peter was a bad husband and father. As an adult, I thought he exhibited the worst traits of American and Central European sexism. I hated the contemptuous way he treated women, his indifference to his children, and the patronizing way he played the role of rich and powerful businessman.

To his credit, Uncle Peter had maintained contact with my parents from the time they arrived in Manhattan until they died. His secretary sent me checks every year for my birthday that I dutifully thanked him for. But after my mother died, I saw him as little as possible. Now, I called him up and, after explaining that I was writing another book, I asked him if he could tell me what he knew about my mother and Ivan.

Of course he knew about their affair! Uncle Peter declaimed into the telephone. It was apparently Milena who had proposed the *ménage à trois.*

That shocked me — even though my mother had told me this the day before I started analysis. She was my nanny, for God's sake! How could she propose this arrangement?

Milena and Ivan were both in love with my mother, Uncle Peter went on, in a tone that implied this was nothing new. Franci had told him so. "I know you must find this counter to your thinking but there's no sense of sin in Central Europe! For the Czechs, marriage is forever and sleeping around, no big deal. They screw around like mad. I didn't know about it when it was going on but I wasn't surprised. Franci told me after it was over."

I was trying so hard to manage my feelings that I forgot to ask if and when the affair ended. He volunteered, "I don't think Kurt ever knew."

Uncle Peter was not what I considered a reliable source, but I had no reason to think he would lie. Was I relieved that my father never knew? Or angry? The love affair had gone on for at least a decade under his nose and Ivan was part of our extended family. He and Milena were our substitute grandparents; we kept celebrating Christmas at their home.

"Kurt was always loyal to his team," Uncle Peter said. "He would have swept streets for his family if he had to."

I remembered Ivan's caption beneath the photo of our family on Silver Point beach. *Lincoln: That's no burden; that's my family.* I also remembered my mother telling me that her unplanned pregnancy with my baby brother had been a sign and symbol. She had not told me then what its significance, I now inferred, had been: the end of her affair with Ivan and her re-commitment to her marriage.

"Franci could not have done any better in terms of a husband," Uncle Peter said. "When she met him after the war in Prague, Kurt was a celebrity and a gentleman. Good family connections meant a lot then. He was Jewish aristocracy from the countryside. His father owned a factory. His relatives owned coal mines and banks. He had been a national swim champion and played water polo in the Olympics.

"He comes back from the concentration camps a survivor, a venerable figure from the dead. They get married. They get a nice apartment. You're born. Then, this flower of civilization is uprooted. They arrive in New York. Everything about his status is eliminated. He can't speak English. He can't do anything in sports or business or the social world. Worst of all, it turns out he has an inability to adapt."

It was difficult but useful to hear this about my father, especially from narcissistic, patronizing Uncle Peter. At the time my father was flailing around trying to find or keep a menial job, Peter was climbing the corporate ladder and living in a posh suburb, to which we were invited on special occasions. I had gotten the impression, even as a little girl, that he distanced himself from the refugee community. He looked down on them. Even on my mother. I had found it painful then and infuriating now. I thanked him for his time and got off the phone as quickly as I decently could.

It was easier and more helpful to talk with people who did not personally know my parents but knew their culture and their experience during the war. Other daughters of Holocaust survivors reminded me of what I had myself written: that Franci had been only 19 when her world was destroyed; in her early twenties when Auschwitz turned her from a human being into a number; how she had tried to commit suicide at 25, but managed to live with overwhelming loss, dislocation, the disappointments of emigration. *Nothing after the war was a big deal,* my brother said. Their tragedy was behind them.

I knew that. I had spent many years interviewing survivors and their children. But I hadn't focused on how the war had affected love, sexuality, pleasure, and the need to be thought desirable. Robbie had tried to push me to think about these things in regard to Franci but I wasn't able to comfortably talk to him — maybe our own relationship was too close to my mother's with Ivan. I couldn't easily talk to Dr. M. about it either: I thought he was the son of a rare, "normal" survivor couple's marriage, and that he was critical not only of my parents but of their entire way of life. I consulted with the Czech women friends I had made over many years of research and writing about my family, women in various professions who brought their perspectives as well as personal experiences to bear in ways I could not.

They pointed out that Ivan and Milena were a generation older than my mother. They embodied Prague culture of the 1920s and 30s, when the city was a magnet for artists and writers, refugees and people on the fringe — much like New York. They came from prominent families. They hob-nobbed with celebrities. And, both of them thought, she was a beautiful woman, when for years she had been nothing more than a number. They fell in love with her. They made her feel human again. And they weren't Jews! They were gentiles who adored her and found her valuable.

That all made sense, I thought. But how was it possible that none of them — especially my nanny — had considered the effect that conducting a love affair in our home would have on me?

My friends said I needed to better imagine the emotional state of the refugees after the war and the poverty of their options for pleasure. They could barely pay their rent. They had no money for hotel rooms or weekends away. None could afford to buy the necessities for discretion. Franci was tied down to her business — she had been the breadwinner after all — and they couldn't have sex in the street or in Central Park. Their flirtations and everything else played out in their homes.

Quite apart from those constraints, I had to understand that Czechs treated children more like pets than people, my friends said. In their experience, parents rarely worried about what they saw or heard.

"I will tell you what happened to me," said my friend Hanka, who grew up in Czechoslovakia and now lived in Toronto. "It affected me so much that I forgot it for many years."

"I was about twelve years old. Mother and I were returning from a visit with my grandmother in Moravia, and got a lift from a friend who I later learned was my mother's lover. They were in the front and I was in the back next to his son, who was about seventeen or eighteen. He kept trying to put his hand up my skirt in a very domineering manner. I kept pushing his hand away, making quite a lot of noise. My mother noticed this and his behavior, but instead of stopping him, she just made some jokes. She brushed the whole thing off as 'funny,' giving the guy a green light to continue. By the time we got to Prague four hours later I was feeling mortified, exhausted, degraded, dirty, violated.

"I was never able to trust my mother again. She thought this kind of behavior was normal, inevitable, acceptable and harmless. For me, it was so traumatic that I forgot it for a very long time. When I finally remembered, I couldn't sleep for weeks, I was so angry and the problem was that I was not allowed to be angry at my parents."

Hearing Hanka describe her experience helped me clarify my own. She had been 12, had a command of the language, an understanding of social norms, and a clear memory of the people and the incident. I had had none of those things. I was wondering yet again whether I should give up and abandon my project when I received an email unrelated to my research. It was from a man I had met as a child but barely knew.

~ 40 ~

"Nazdar Helenko," or *"Hi, Helenka,"* read the email. *"I hope we can establish contact again. I need some advice."* He signed it, *"Your former babysitter, Jan Drábek."*

I remembered his name and his mother.

Jan was a Prague-born journalist in his 70s who lived in Vancouver, British Columbia. He was looking for an American literary agent. I knew that his parents had been friends of my parents, and that his tidy, exacting mother Mrs. Drábková — who had preceded Milena as my nanny — had managed to toilet train me at the age of 12 months. If anyone was obsessively concerned with cleanliness or cleared the dinner table too quickly, one of my parents would laugh and say to the other, *"Drábková!"*

I sent Jan some names of agents. Then I asked if he could fill me in on his early years in America.

We were soon talking over the phone. Jan's father had been a prominent lawyer in Prague and, like Ivan, among the non-Jews arrested after Hitler invaded the city. Mr. Drábek had been deported to Auschwitz as a political prisoner and became one of the rare men to be taken out of the camp by the Gestapo and not returned. After the war ended, Mr. Drábek had prosecuted Nazis for war crimes. He also was a staunch anti-Communist, advised to flee after the Communist take-over of 1948. Like Ivan and Milena, the Drábeks had crossed the border on skis, with only what they could carry on their backs.

Like the others Czech refugees in my parents' circle, they were highly-educated, middle-class people with no English, no money, and no prospects for employment. The Czech obstetrician who served as the hub of the émigré community sent Mrs. Drábková to work as a seamstress for my mother. But, Jan said, his mother adored me and preferred babysitting to sewing. Occasionally, Jan also babysat, spending the night at the Epsteins' basement apartment.

I asked Jan to describe it.

There were three small rooms, a kitchen and a bathroom, he said: my mother's workroom; the bedroom where I slept in a crib beside my parents' bed; and the living room/*salon* where customers had their fittings, and where he had slept on the couch.

Remembering my own nights babysitting, I asked what he had thought about my parents.

"Your parents seemed happy to me," he said. "I thought your father was great. The sports stories. The Olympics. He talked to me seriously even though I was just a teenager. Of course — like with most newly arrived immigrants — there was the stress of trying to make it in a new land."

Jan volunteered that he had several boxes of his father's papers in his basement and felt sure that there was stuff about my family in them, including photographs. It hadn't mattered who worked for whom or what anyone had been in Prague: all of them were poor, in exile, and took every opportunity to socialize together in New York. I was one of the few babies in the refugee community and a very pretty, charming little girl. He began sending me photographs.

I had seen most of them before but one was new to me.

This was not one of Ivan's well-composed photographs, but a cluttered snapshot probably taken by my father. As I examined the happy toddler in a bathtub, engaged with her attentive nanny, my eyes went behind them to the rather ordinary fixtures on the tile wall. I recognized them as the ones I had tried to draw that morphed into genitals.

I enlarged the shot, tried to sharpen its details, and fill in what was missing in the picture: the door, the lock, the places where Ivan and my mother might have sat or stood together. We had lived in that apartment until I was three and a half, until my brother's birth.

When I called to thank Jan, I asked how well he had known Ivan and Milena, who succeeded his mother as my nanny.

Very well, he told me. His father and Ivan had been good friends. "But Father was a straight arrow while Ivan was a wild man. He was known as a womanizer and even tried to seduce my mother. She tolerated him because he had been on the right side as far as Nazism and Communism went. Besides, everything was tolerated back then."

Seemingly, I thought.

"As a teenager, I was impressed by Ivan," Jan told me. "He would say 'shit' and 'Go fuck yourself.' My mother tried to keep me and my brother away from him because of his language. I remember that he wanted to write a book about the war and call it *Shit on the Graves and No Chrysanthemums.* You know, the kind of language teenage boys are impressed by."

Mrs. Drábková sounded as though she was the only Czech with a sense of propriety. I wondered whether I had understood that Ivan had been a verbally vulgar man. Certainly I had found him sleazy. I said to Jan, trying hard to sound casual, that he must have known that my mother had been in love with Ivan.

There was a silence over the line worthy of Dr. M. He asked how I knew and I told him about my lunch with Franci on the day before I started psychoanalysis 30 years before.

"According to my mother," Jan continued, "it was common knowledge that they were having an affair. Ivan used to brag that your mother was the most beautiful woman in New York City. We thought Milena was a saint. She had to be a saint to stay with him."

Another silence. Then, "Shortly after it came out, I read your book *Children of Holocaust.* My mother was still alive and I remember discussing it with her. She said you must have been too young to notice, but it was a shame you didn't know any better than to describe him as a benign grandfather."

She had pitied me, I thought with a mix of anger and relief. At least one person in that dislocated, demoralized group disapproved of the situation that Ivan and my mother had created. It was bracing to hear the prim lawyer's wife's words from the grave via her son. A kind of posthumous character witness, I thought. Over the years, I had interviewed the surviving members of my parents' community about them. Almost all described my mother as smart, elegant, and pragmatic — a woman whose business kept the family financially afloat. They described my father as a sportsman of the old school, idealistic, fair, gentlemanly. One man had even told me he thought my father had been stupid — a remark that had startled and hurt me. I had tried to forget it but it had remained in my mind.

I didn't confide in my one-time babysitter Jan about the extent of Ivan's malevolence. Instead I thanked him for his unexpected help. I believed all the testimony I had elicited from other people. I needed to believe my own.

~ 41 ~

As I learned in many different venues, childhood trauma has an extraordinarily long and resilient half-life. Close to my sixtieth birthday, I was still learning how deeply its consequences colored my perceptions, my reactions, even my writing process. Like Penelope at her loom, I kept unraveling what I stitched together. My computer facilitated impulsive cutting and editing. I even deleted or repeatedly misfiled whole chapters so inventively that I couldn't recover them. I learned to back up my back ups, print out chapters I had completed. I emailed them to myself and to friends so that when I erased what I had written, it wouldn't vanish.

As that struggle between knowing and not knowing impeded my writing process, I continued to work with Dr. M. twice a week. My focus remained fierce and some of my oldest friends tired of my doubling back over the same subjects over and over again. They didn't understand my erratic, difficult connection with Robbie or why therapy was taking so long. I felt they were abandoning me when I needed them.

My husband remained his unconditionally loving, uxorious self while allowing me to work alone. I had chosen a spouse, I finally understood, who shared the absolute self-confidence, integrity, and optimism of my late father, along with his ethical standards. Though Kurt had been an athlete and Patrick was more of a scientist/engineer, they shared a rock-hard idealism and commitment to family.

Robbie and the men I fell for before my husband, I understood, were more like my mother: emotional, intellectually intriguing, artistic, unhindered by the notion of boundaries. I had played the role of their sympathetic audience and loyal supporter for most of my life. The difference now, after years of trying to understand what had gone on, was that I now understood what I brought to the table.

The old intensity of what I had sometimes felt as a mystical connection to Robbie diminished. Our relation would, I suspected, never feel ordinary to me, but as I told Dr. M., it was becoming "normal."

Nearly six years into therapy, I still preferred long-distance to in-person sessions. I was unaware that part of me was still frightened of being alone in a room with him. But I thought it important to see him in person every few months, and to revisit the city, walk through my childhood haunts, see my brothers and friends, go to museums, concerts, the theater.

In November of 2006, I took the subway to the Brooklyn Museum's Annie Leibovitz exhibit, *A Photographer's Life.* I was familiar with her celebrity portraits in vivid color. I had not seen her more intimate, black-and-white shots of her family — especially of her mother and father, and her lover, Susan Sontag. She had photographed Sontag, alive, in Venice, Paris and Sarajevo, ill and then deceased in New York City.

As I examined the photographs, I grew uneasy about the photographer's intrusion in the name of art. In some cultures, I remembered, taking a photograph was seen as stealing a soul: repulsive and forbidden.

As I examined the photographs of a woman artist who, I knew, was not only of my generation but very tall, I identified both with her and the objects of her gaze. I was acutely aware of another kind of split: I was the helpless woman in the photographs on show but I was also, as Ivan had captioned himself in his album, the Author.

That evening, I went to see a play in a small, experimental theater. A male actor holding a microphone gave instructions to a female actor who had not been given a script, whose role was to simply do what he said. It affected me like a strange dream. Not until much later did I recall Ivan's microphone and old reel-to-reel tape recorder. He had taped me singing American and Czech folk songs for one of his Radio Free Europe broadcasts as a 15-year-old. He had still been an intimate part of my family's life when I was 15! And I, so cleverly disguised as a forthright, sunny teenager, was still keeping secrecy and silence. How on earth, I wondered, had my parents managed their feelings?

The next day, I greeted Dr. M. with my usual smile, sat down in my usual chair, and pressed "Record" on the tape recorder that was now a routine part of our sessions. His office seemed less claustrophobic to me, and I wondered aloud if my sense of ample space meant therapy had become more comfortable.

As soon as I said that, Poe's *The Pit and the Pendulum* rolled into my mind again, the walls closing in on the helpless prisoner of the Inquisition. I was able to articulate this to Dr. M. and moved on to an equally sinister association, the movie *Fantasia,* the especially frightening part where the Sorcerer's broomsticks start multiplying. I became aware of my throat feeling parched.

"I need some water," I hear my voice on the recording. "Do you have any water?"

Unexpectedly, Dr. M. reached under his desk and produced a small bottle of water.

"Thank you," I said politely, though his sudden gesture had rattled me as much as his closing the blinds. I unscrewed the bottle cap, and raised the bottle to my lips, then stopped dead.

Watching him watching me, I was acutely aware that the bottle was the size and shape of a penis. It seemed so obvious and yet so necessary to pretend it was not. Something happened in my body and I did a version of splitting.

"You don't have a cup?" I heard myself ask, trying to sound casual.

When he shook his head, I got up and bolted out of the room. I remembered paper cups in his washroom and returned with one in my hand. I sat down again, carefully poured the water into it, took a sip and, trying to erase everything that had just happened, said, "So, what else?"

"Well, what about what you just said?"

I have no idea what I just said. I emit a sound somewhere between a groan and a sob and then Dr. M. — bless him in these moments — lets out one of his chuckles. That relaxes me enough to say, "The metaphorical is problematical. It's just too close."

He waits for me to go on. I try very hard to speak in a casual way, as though I'm discussing nothing more loaded than the weather.

"I guess what just happened in terms of the bottle was aversion. I just didn't want to do anything that was associated with a penis in my mouth."

"So would the fear be that I might ask you to put my penis in your mouth?"

That made me feel like bolting out of the room again but I heard myself say calmly, "I thought about it, but I don't think so."

Really? I think when I listen to the recording or read my summary of the session. How can I possibly not think so?

Dissociation and denial were my only options. To admit the possibility that Dr. M. might want me to give him a blowjob made my skin crawl. He might be a good man like my father but he might also be a bad man like Ivan. How could I know for sure?

On the recording, my effort to dissociate is clear. I babble, obfuscate. "There's something about taking the bottle and drinking it in front of you. I don't want to do it. The metaphor and the memory... I just want to avoid it. It must have to do with some transferential thing..."

"Well, that was vague," Dr. M. says, after a pause.

I want to say, "I'm showing you something that happened. I don't know whether you're like Ivan or my father."

But I say nothing. If Dr. M. is like Ivan, he terrifies me. If he is like my father I want to protect him. I don't want him to see anything. My recording breaks off abruptly so I don't know how our session ends.

I thought I was upset, but more or less all right. My plan was to return home by train after the session. I took a series of subways to Penn Station without any problem. I got there, bought a ticket and sat down in the waiting area for what should have been half an hour. I thought I kept an eye on the large clock near my seat, but must have gone into an altered state, because I missed my train. When I realized it, I demanded to know from the information desk why there hadn't been an announcement.

"They made three announcements, lady," said the clerk. "One hundred and forty-two passengers got on that train."

I renegotiated my ticket and walked around the station, taking deep breaths of the stale air. I called Patrick. He didn't think it was a big deal; there'd be another train in an hour. He'd pick me up then. But when I hung up, it occurred to me that this was an emergency, and that I should call Dr. M. He didn't pick up his telephone but, for the first time, I left a message telling him that I was in trouble and needed an emergency session.

"You had a traumatic experience," he said, the next day.

Why hadn't he noticed when I left his office? How could he have let me leave in the state I was in? Or had he missed it? What kind of doctor was he?

"You looked a lot less upset than you were."

"Didn't it occur to you in session that I was upset?"

"I didn't have any idea," he says. "I thought you were joking."

Joking? The poet Stevie Smith's lines came to mind: "I was much too far out... and not waving but drowning."

Was I so accomplished a dissembler that he couldn't, after years of working with me, see through me?

"What amazes me," I say out loud, "is the struggle between what I'm feeling and what I allow other people to see." To myself I said: what kind of patient persists in acting as though everything's fine when it's not?

"Maybe you have a sense of shame about it."

That was the first time Dr. M. decided to use the word but it was still premature: I wasn't willing yet to acknowledge shame. Instead I told him how sick I was of my excavation of the past and how futile the enterprise of analysis felt. I felt hopeless about being believed both then, as a child, and now, as an adult. I had no witnesses, the accuracy of memory was being challenged from all sides and recording my sessions only proved how imperfect my own memory was.

On the recording, I hear myself voice a fear that's been on my mind for a long time:

"I'm afraid you think I imagined all of this and that it's what happened to my mother in the war: Helen's mother was raped during the war; Helen's mother told her about rape therefore little Helen in the subways was worried about being raped. But I don't think that's true."

"But you think that's what I think?"

"Yes."

"Why?" He sounds truly surprised.

"Because you've said it in various ways."

"That wouldn't be a very psychoanalytic way of understanding things."

"Then what *do* you think?"

Dr. M. lets a moment go by. Then, in his neutral tone, he says "I know that one setting or complex of feelings permeate many different experiences and situations for you."

The actor with the microphone I saw at the theater comes into my mind again and I use the play to help me formulate what I need to say and can't.

"There're lots of things that connect to that man. First, there's Ivan telling me what to do and my just doing it. That connects to being photographed and being told how to pose. But the hypnotist also has to do with you — I always listen to your voice in a way that gives you authority, wondering: is this true or not true? Is this real or is this not real? Did this happen or did this not happen?"

“I don’t mean that fantasy can’t come from real experience,” Dr. M. says slowly. “So in my office you were able to maintain some external composure at the same time that your internal experience was highly fueled by fantasy, which may have been based on real experience.”

I try to understand this and give up.

“Right,” I say, “but whatever it is, it’s really, really upsetting. And I don’t think it’s about my mother’s war experience!”

A buzz cuts across the recording and I hear him say, “We have to stop.”

When I listen to myself, I’m struck by how I’m still throwing dust in my eyes, acting things out rather than naming them, leaning on other people’s stories rather than telling my own. I’m grateful to be living in the 21st century when so many stories that were suppressed are being told and shown, but impatient with myself. How much longer will it take me, I wonder, before I can say what I mean.

~ 42 ~

I turned sixty at the end of 2007, aware of how much the world had changed over my lifetime. The first African-American man and the first white woman were vying for the Democratic Presidential candidacy. My state of Massachusetts had become the first state in America to legalize same-sex marriage. Thanks to the investigative journalists of the *Boston Globe* and public interest in the Catholic Church scandal, it had become easier for men and women everywhere in the world to speak and write about sexual molestation.

I was acutely aware of changes at home too. My sons were now young men, the older one interviewing for his first job; the younger one at music conservatory. Patrick and I were home alone. With only my therapy tethering me to a schedule. I heard myself asking, like a child on a car trip, "Are we there yet?"

Dr. M. didn't answer at first. Eventually he said, "For much of your life, your feelings were dissociated from your experience. Many of those feelings were sexual. Has that changed? Does it still happen?"

I didn't answer Dr. M. out loud. I thought through my answers in silence, connecting the dots into lines I hadn't drawn before. Despite my periodic bouts of impatience with myself and Dr. M., I knew many things had changed, particularly dissociative habits which had served me well in some cases and very badly in others.

If I had been able to compose a cogent reply to Dr. M.'s question, I would have begun by saying that I hadn't left my body in a very long time, but I was well aware that dissociation and denial were my default mechanisms of defense against pain. I was a very good person to have around in an emergency; I acted effectively, unencumbered by feeling. I had also come to think of dissociation as a professional asset for a journalist, especially in situations of danger. I was not a war reporter but I used my ability to dissociate regularly during interviews, when people talked about painful subjects, or when I spoke in public about things that caused me pain. I was also aware of dissociating from painful content when I wrote. So I had come to think of the technique as a form of resilience as well as a problem.

Of course my dissociation of sexual feelings had changed over time. According to researchers, all children experience sexual feelings and sensations but I could remember none — not even when I acted out *Peyton Place* with my friend Laura. I told Dr. M. about an experience at a summer camp dance when I was 11 or maybe 12. My partner was a boy about my height. It was a slow dance, we were barely moving, when suddenly a lump formed between us. It became uncomfortable, then scary. Was it happening, I wondered, or was I imagining it?

When the music stopped, we walked off the wooden platform and sat down under a tree. I liked the boy. I wanted to talk to him. I wanted to tell him that he looked like a boy I knew, but something had gone wrong with my brain and all I could manage was, "You look like a boy." I had been so mortified by what I said that I forgot everything that happened afterwards. But I remembered the incident half a century later.

In the same way, I remembered the delivery boy who followed me into my elevator. He pressed me into the pock-marked wall and tried to kiss me. I had first frozen, then fled, down several flights of stairs and out into the street.

I had to work out in my writing, without Dr. M., over and over again, writing and reading what I had written, how those boys of my childhood and adolescence were connected to Ivan. As a small child, I hadn't had a language in which to describe how Ivan was bothering me. As far as the way men in the city bothered girls and women, neither did the culture in which I grew up. My coping mechanism — and an effective one for the situations at hand — had been to dissociate all of it.

It hadn't been until high school when I reaped the results. I was awkward with boys, unfamiliar with sexual pleasure and ashamed of being what my best friend called "a sexual retard." Instead of feeling pleased with my body and the attention it drew, I had felt targeted and anxious. Dissociation explained why I had felt nothing when I tried to "get experience" in the car with Michael, nothing when I lost my virginity, why I left my body when I slept with Robbie.

I sometimes wondered whether my tendency was inherited, an example of bio-chemical, epigenetic change. Or, whether I had learned to adapt my mother's strategy to cope with her suicide threats, and live with the wolf in my house. In any case, I told my analyst, my tendencies toward dissociation had changed a great deal. They no longer troubled me.

When had I become aware of my dissociation around sex changing? That was also too tied up with shame and other people's secrets to tell Dr. M. I preferred to write it out in private and put it between the covers of a book where it had a life separate from mine. After finally learning how to masturbate at 23, I grasped how my body and mind worked together to produce varieties of pleasure and orgasm. Yet despite much practice and an unsuccessful encounter with another woman, my body remained dead to sensation with a partner.

Then, when I was 25 and pursuing freelance assignments, a fellow journalist sent me to an editor at *Penthouse,* then a brand-new men's magazine. I felt guilty about even considering calling him. It was 1973 — the height of second-wave feminism. At that time, *Penthouse* was not a name I would drop casually into conversation with my friends. But I did call the editor and we had a very long expense-account lunch.

Tall, brusque, and only a couple of years older than myself, Francis had just been hired away from the *New York Times* and tasked with attracting investigative reporters to *Penthouse.* He was dead serious about what seemed to me a bogus mission. Did I have any article ideas?

I had said I was not a *Penthouse* reader, so couldn't imagine what kind of investigative piece he had in mind.

Would it interest me to do a piece on premature ejaculation? It was the number one problem, based on surveys, bothering *Penthouse* readers.

Knowing what I know now about my dissociative style, I'm sure I took that information in stride. I remember smiling and saying that I hadn't had much sexual experience and hadn't thought at all about premature ejaculation. It sounded like a good idea if his readers were preoccupied by the problem — but it wasn't a good fit for me.

Francis seemed to appreciate the candor of my answer. He asked what I liked to write about. When I answered that I was researching the effects of trauma on children of Holocaust survivors, he volunteered that his own parents were in that group. Before lunch was over, I learned that his Viennese parents had been imprisoned in a British internment camp for enemy aliens; that — like my mother — he had been named for the Austrian Emperor Franz Josef; and that his marriage was ending.

Over the next year, though I never took an assignment to write for *Penthouse* and we dated other people, we became good friends. I learned that we not only shared a cultural background. His parents never recovered from their internment and lived as displaced people for the rest of their lives. During one of the most traumatic episodes in his childhood, as a five-year-old, he had been raped by a stranger.

At the time, I didn't grasp the relevance of his experience to my own life. No friend until then had ever confided that he or she had been sexually assaulted as a child and, though I don't remember him asking me to, I kept the information secret.

I had listened closely, filed the information deep down inside me and told no one about it.

Looking back, I find it no coincidence that Francis was the man whom I eventually trusted enough to engage in sex for which I was fully present. One evening at his apartment we talked into the next day and finally lay down on his bed. Once there, I had felt comfortable telling him that I wasn't ready to have sex. We lay in one another's arms for a long time without speaking, and eventually went to sleep. Only the next morning, after he asked whether I was sure I wanted to, did we have sex.

I wasn't then conscious of how his sexual history had played a role in our relationship but, even then, was moved by the fact that he had been wounded and then healed.

Robbie had had trouble accepting my relationship with a man who edited a soft-porn magazine. He called our time together my "glam phase" and my boyfriend "Porn Man." Our domicile was glamorous too, an all-white, hi-tech Village studio, with no kitchen and little furniture but a queen-sized bed. Everything about that time and place seemed frozen in time.

To Dr. M.'s question about whether my dissociation of sexual matters had changed, I could therefore say yes, definitely. I was no longer frozen in time. My sexual radar was operative: I was now able to identify and enjoy sexual attraction and even to flirt a bit. But, at 60, I was still uneasy in social situations about the border between playing at seduction and acting on it. I still found myself disturbed, not delighted, by seductive behavior — even when it was directed toward me by good friends, even when I watched it directed at other people, not me.

I regret that. Given my adventuresome nature, I might have become a *femme fatale.* Instead, flirting felt like a game too dangerous for me to play. Until inexcusably late, I had been willfully obtuse when a man came on to me. I've saved a souvenir of that bold but baffling young woman: a vial of Chanel Number 5, whose meaning I ignored when it was presented to me decades ago by a middle-aged, married man hoping to seduce me.

My own middle age moved me from the object of attraction to the periphery. I'm content to be there. When an over-fond man moves to kiss me or rest his arm on my body, I have no problem stepping away. Unlike so many women I know, I'm grateful when a male gaze does not rest on me. I finally feel close to invisible.

I wish I had been able to say all of this to Dr. M. when I was his analysand. But it took more time and space to formulate and I hope he reads it here.

~ 43 ~

As my analyst and I headed toward the finish line in the spring of 2008, I began reading up on what psychoanalysts call "termination." A good ending, I read, was determined not only by the therapeutic pair, but by their history of other significant endings. It was a good thing, I thought, that Dr. M. had regular experience of this; endings were usually torturous for me. The word termination sounded uncomfortably like extermination to me.

Did ending therapy have to mean losing Dr. M.? As a professor, I had had many students. Some of those students had become friends after graduation. Of course, I knew that the conventions of psychoanalysis differed from those of college but I was a rebel against established rules.

Dr. M. did not, at first, pick up on my comments about ending therapy. He seemed to think I still had work to do, particularly around the issue of anger: at Ivan for molesting me; at my mother and father for allowing it to happen; at my two brothers, at Robbie, at himself and at most men.

Wasn't writing a memoir a form of revenge? Dr. M. asked, and I didn't, in fact, get angry. He had probably never read a memoir in his life! What would he know about why writers wrote them?

Memoirs could be vehicles of revenge and revenge could be one of the many reasons prompting a book. But there were plenty of other reasons to write a memoir, including the opposite of revenge: to immortalize a beloved person or event, to draw attention to a forgotten life or relationship, to mourn, celebrate or teach.

"I'm talking about your memoir," said Dr. M.

I replied with my reasons for writing: to look back and try to make sense of something painful or puzzling in my life; to set the record straight; to bear witness where there had been no witness. Many experiences left out of or banned from public discourse were first expressed in memoir. I thought that putting into words what had not been said before and holding up a mirror to the reader was difficult but essential work, far from revenge. I had experienced its benevolent power when I wrote about children of Holocaust survivors.

Good memoirs revisited life experience in search of something troubling and elusive and educated both writer and reader in the process. I hadn't set out to write about Ivan or my mother — I had started out wanting to understand what had happened to me as a young woman with Robbie. Working with him and uncovering my early childhood drama felt less like revenge than reclamation.

Dr. M. said nothing. Then, "What about your brothers?" asked Dr. M.

I remembered that my analyst was a younger brother.

"They don't have much to do with this story," I said with some impatience. I knew he put great stock in sibling rivalry and was sure I had felt displaced and angry when my brother Tommy was born. We had spent time discussing the craziness of my mother scheduling my tonsillectomy to coincide with her delivery but, really, my feelings about the arrival of a younger sibling were dwarfed by the other elements of my situation.

I knew that Dr. M. wanted me to see as complete a picture of the circumstances as I could but I had begun to tire of our endless consideration of what were beginning to seem like tangents. The truth was that I was finally getting sick and tired of talking about my childhood and what Ivan did or did not do to my mother and to me. I didn't care about the specifics anymore. I knew that something had happened, that it had happened not once but over a period of several years, and that I had had to accept Ivan's presence in our family without complaint, as if I didn't know any of what I knew.

There was no doubt in my mind about that anymore.

In those last months with Dr. M. I began to challenge his comments and questions more, treat our sessions more like conversations with friends. My relations with my brothers were okay, I said, no better or worse than sibling relationships I knew about from friends.

As far as displacing my anger at Ivan onto objectionable men — of which I saw far too many — I *did* often become enraged when confronted with bullying, but saw it as a good if sometimes risky thing. When I misunderstood a detour sign and the policeman directing traffic came up to my car window and yelled at me, I thought he was behaving abusively and told him so. I still remembered my outrage, 25 years earlier, when, pregnant and driving my minivan, I was pulled over by a state trooper for not slowing down for a blinking yellow light late at night. I remembered my blindness when he beamed his flashlight into my eyes, and berated me. I was enraged by the way everyone had to kowtow to policemen. It wasn't hard to understand how much more enraging and humiliating it was for people of color.

Yes, I would be a better and safer human being if I could better control those feelings of rage. Maybe one day I would be able to notice them and let them go as prescribed in yoga class. But, for the moment, I was glad to feel, glad to be angry in real time.

I was also glad to feel rage when I read about yet another man in power — a politician or entertainer or corporate executive — who had used his position of power for sexual exploitation. And I continued to be enraged at my friend's former therapist, still in practice in Massachusetts, years after I had first told Dr. M. about him and my analyst had blurted, "Report him." The good news was that my friend had, with the encouragement of her husband and friends like myself, finally filed a complaint with the

Massachusetts Licensing Board, since only she had the legal standing to do it.

I could understand my story more easily now: I had been sexually molested by Ivan as a child and probably told to keep his and my mother's secret. I was taught, above all, that adults might abuse children but that well-brought-up children did not offend adults. In adolescence, I had admired boys who defied authority to the point of dropping out of the established system. Old classmates remembered me as a rebel myself. When I look over records from journalism school, I realize that I almost did not graduate because I challenged almost every professor.

Well, seven years of psychoanalysis had helped explain why. I understood the sources of my anger now and could modulate my reactions — not always, not perfectly, just better.

But rage, I told Dr. M., had never plagued me with the persistence or varieties of problems that doubt presented: doubt, self-doubt, guilt and shame for retaining a naïveté well past the usual time frame had been far larger problems. They had made me unable to trust my perceptions of people and situations. Though my powers of observation were razor-sharp, they could easily be fogged by the memory of past trauma.

My analyst was a thorough professional and as strong-willed as I but, eventually, he asked what my thoughts were about a termination date. In July of 2008, I said August, maybe before his annual vacation.

He said nothing.

"How about my birthday — end of November."

Dr. M. said, "That's more realistic."

In August, Dr. M. and I both went on vacation. I questioned friends about termination. Some had never left therapy; others had done so in anger or disappointment. Dr. M. kept saying that termination was not as final as it sounded, that I could always return for treatment. But I didn't want to return for treatment; I wanted to graduate and put what had brought me into therapy to final rest.

In October, I wondered aloud to Dr. M. whether we could have an exit interview. I elicited no response. I then told him how I conceived of termination as graduation, which included a celebratory meal at a Manhattan restaurant like Café Sabarsky in the Neue Galerie of Austrian Art.

"Why Café Sabarsky?"

"Eating well is the best revenge," came to mind. The café was one of the only places left in Manhattan that served the kind of food I ate as a child. It was a short walk from his office and it overlooked Central Park. Many of the paintings in the museum were of girls and women objectified and sexualized by Klimt, Kokoschka, and Schiele — Central European men with more than a passing resemblance to Ivan. Celebrating at Café Sabarsky would be a multi-layered symbol of a successful therapy. Just desserts. On the menu were the *sachertorte* and *apfelstrudel* I had loved to eat as a child.

Dr. M. nixed Café Sabarsky. What if someone recognized him? How would he introduce me? I found these responses lame but didn't argue. He was a scrupulous man, hewing strictly to professional practice. Given my history, given the situation of my friend and her therapist, why would I want him to do anything else? But I did and had to make peace with the fact that he made no exception to his rules.

In November, however, with only five sessions left to go, we had an altercation. I told him that I'd been talking about termination with other psychoanalysts and was frustrated that I couldn't have the same kind of discussion with him. I couldn't understand the logic of not having an exit interview, in which we would compare notes. Analyzing down to the wire in our one-way manner felt to me like driving off a cliff. I explained my idea of an exit interview once again and said his refusal to even talk about it made me feel as though I were being forced into his way of doing things.

"And you want to force me into your way of doing things," Dr. M. replied. My proposal of an exit interview, he said, was not an analytic session.

He said it in his usual even tone so I didn't realize, at first, that he was angry.

"Well no," I replied. I hadn't thought of it as me interviewing him but as a summary from us both. "I didn't dream up the practice of exit interviews," I said. "They're done in many professions."

"But a summary with what parameters? Along what dimensions? What kind of summary could you possibly give me that you wouldn't have said already?"

"Well, for me, it's important to think about the whole seven years as an entity. Especially since they're ending."

"Especially since you're going to be writing about it," Dr. M. said.

Was that why he brought up revenge? Was I obligated to think about his feelings? Was he worried about how he would appear in print? Was confidentiality a one-way or two-way street?

"I think you're trying to bully me," Dr. M. continued, "I think you're trying to intimidate me, saying nobody else does it this way. I can't believe that you're being so bullying — don't you see that enactment?"

"No," I said.

"Well that's what it is. Didn't you poll people to determine that my dealing with you is abnormal? You have a consensus of people who agree with you. You're trying to get me to talk. Why don't you — you know, just twist my arm, why don't you get me to... You're coming on like a complete bully."

What was going on with my analyst? I wondered.

"I think you might have an agenda that you're unaware of," he insisted. "Or certainly that you're not telling me about."

"How can I tell you about an agenda I'm not aware I have."

"That you don't have, or you're not aware of?"

"That I think that I don't have. That you think that I'm unaware of."

I had never before felt as though Dr. M. was shoving an interpretation down my throat. Now I did. When he called me a bully yet again, I tried my best to control my anger and to point out, mildly, "I don't see how disagreeing with you is behaving like a bully."

"Because your methods are bullying. You demand. You make fun of the profession. You try to intimidate me to do your will."

That was 32 minutes into the session that I played and replayed over and over again in the last and final weeks of my analysis. I had wondered for so long what Dr. M. was really like. Now I got a glimpse. I didn't dissociate, but took in his words and tone of voice, and monitored my growing anger until he said, "We have to stop. So we speak on Monday?"

"I don't know." I said sarcastically. "It depends if you're correct and I find this hour valuable, or a complete waste of time."

"Usually when we've had a session like this, the next session is helpful to evaluate."

I canceled my next session. After a few days, I wrote my analyst a long letter. I wrote him that I had experienced our nearly eight years of work as an extraordinary and interesting spiritual adventure. *"However painful and austere, whatever our ups and downs,"* I wrote, *"I was always buoyed up by a sense of mutual respect and collaboration. So I was pretty devastated by our last session, which I experienced as a nightmare."*

I compared him to famous men in fact and fiction whom I viewed as authoritarian: Freud, determined to prove his brilliance to Dora; Professor Higgins bullying Eliza. I described Nora walking out on her pompous patriarchal husband in *A Doll's House.* But those literary representations were for his use — not mine. I didn't need the scaffolding of other people's stories anymore. If his intent had been to elicit my rage, I wrote, he had succeeded. To what end? I hadn't imagined this kind of ending, not its suddenness or violence or hurt, and I was trying to understand how it happened.

I wrote about how deeply sad I was about ending analysis and how difficult it had been for me to figure out how to do it. I thought it was probably difficult for him too.

But I pointed out that analysis with all its benefits was an authoritarian relationship with rigid rules. *"That closely replicates my relationship with my parents,"* I wrote, *"and I was hoping, that we could end by moving to a more egalitarian paradigm."*

Meeting behind a closed door with a male authority figure also evoked my situation of being alone with Ivan. I had been able to subsume (or dissociate) those parallels until now but I was unwilling to continue doing it. I felt I had grown up.

I stood firm on my wish to end by the end of the year. Dr. M. stood firm about not changing how we worked. We set our termination date for December 18. The day before our last session, his assistant called to cancel.

"Family emergency," she said.

I was sure that someone in his family had died and thought it had to be Dr. M.'s older sister. I searched the internet for her name and, after a few days, found her obituary. Her decline, just as I was terminating, would explain my analyst's unusual behavior, I thought. I felt sad for him and confused. I didn't think of him as a brother, but suspected that Dr. M. sometimes confused me with his older sister and I felt sorry to be inflicting yet another loss on him.

On December 31, I dialed his number for what I thought would be our last session and told him I knew what had happened. I was able to express my concern for him and also my wish to finish on schedule. I wanted to be done. But somehow we were not yet done and decided that we would end on the second day of 2009.

On January 2, I conducted my own exit interview. I surveyed the state of my marriage, my family, my friendships, my professional life and said that there was nothing left that I couldn't handle by myself. Dr. M. listened and even answered a question or two before he said, "We have to stop."

"Okay," I replied, getting teary.

"So I gather that this is our last session." he said.

"Do you feel comfortable with that?" I asked.

“I’m comfortable with that.” Then, after what sounded like a gulp. “Good luck to you.”

I thought about saying that I had come to love him, that he had become a part of my life that I would deeply miss. Instead, I said, “It’s really, really hard to say good-bye. I’m very glad I came back to work with you and grateful.”

“Thank you,” he said, his voice cracking. “It was a great experience for me as well.”

~ 44 ~

That was the end of my psychoanalytic chapter but not the end of sorting through and trying to absorb my story. For seven years, I wrote and rewrote this book, revision after revision as I made deeper connections between people and events and their significance.

Ivan and Milena, my mother and father, and Robbie were intricately joined in a web I had spun so tightly that, at times, it had paralyzed me. But by the summer of 2016, seventeen years after I called Robbie for help, I had disentangled many of its threads.

Robbie's writing his own memoir now and I am helping him. He remains one of the most significant people in my life, even now that the intensity of our interactions has finally cooled. I no longer need him to be my archive, memory or muse. The sound of his voice on the phone still delights me — we're almost always interested in what the other has to say — and I no longer feel anxious that he'll disappear. We're both old people now and, after decades of misunderstandings, I finally understand our long dance of intimacy and absence.

Some of my friends have asked how I feel about Ivan and if I can't remember exactly what happened, how do I make peace with not knowing?

I would have liked to have discovered a confession from Ivan in the course of my research. Maybe a diary entry that read: *I molested the daughter of my closest friends, Helena, when she was a very small child. I took advantage of my position in the Epstein household as her nanny's husband and her mother's lover. Nothing excuses my behavior. Not even my six years in concentration camp.*

That would have "saved me a lot of time," as my mother so memorably told me decades before. It would have removed all trace of doubt from my mind, supplied unequivocal proof of what I remembered. Perhaps that would have made things easier for me. But it also would have cut short long overdue hours getting to know myself and the reasons I think and feel and act as I do. It also would have curtailed my understanding of the millions of other women and men who have had experiences similar to mine.

Other friends question me about how I've ended up feeling toward my mother. As a wife and mother, how do I understand her reckless and careless disregard for her young children and husband? Why do I think she confessed to me when I was 31, the age she had been during the affair, the day before I began my psychoanalysis? Was she worried that she had made it impossible for me to marry and forfeited her chance of grandchildren? Was confession her way of finally giving me permission to tell someone about it?

I don't have answers to those questions.

What about the lasting effects of sexual abuse? Do I still think of penises each time I see a bathtub spout or a phallic vegetable? Have I made peace with my sexual history? What helped me?

The quarantine I imposed on discussing my therapy and writing, I think in retrospect, was a brilliant idea. It allowed me to be grounded in easy and regular domestic routines. I swam every day and began doing yoga. When the weather was good, I walked miles with my husband and our dog. For the most part, I stopped seeing and dreaming about phallic vegetables and bathroom fixtures, but sometimes I still do.

Almost everyone wants to know where I am on the spectrum of forgiveness. Can I imagine ever forgiving Ivan — or Milena or my mother and father. Why do I imply that their experiences in the war mitigate what happened to me? So what if Ivan was in solitary confinement for two years? So what if my mother's self-esteem was destroyed in the war? You can always find psychological or social reasons for the behavior of perpetrators and bystanders. Abuse and sexual assault of children happen in every community, they say, in war or peace, among rich and poor.

These are difficult questions to answer. The villain of my story has been dead for over 50 years. The other players are also dead. I'm now more than twice as old as my mother was when she fell in love with Ivan and have spent nearly 20 years of therapy trying to untangle a drama that is history. Now that I've lived with the story every day for nearly two decades, I want to close the book, put it behind me, stop obsessing about whether what I know in my bones can be verified.

I don't believe that suffering confers rights but I can now imagine how bitterly Franci railed against the war and immigration: the first stole her identity as a young, beautiful woman; the second obliged her to take on what were then the obligations of a man. Ivan thought she was beautiful, brilliant, sexy. She was good at dissociating; she went for it.

Do I excuse her? No. But I understand her.

As for Milena and my father, the bystanders who either knew and did nothing or — somehow — didn't know, that's about dissociation too. They were all in mourning. They were all scrambling to live in a new country. I think my brother Tommy is right: nothing measured up to what they had experienced.

And, finally, how did my excavation into the past affect my marriage?

It tested my marriage and forced me to examine its strong and weak spots. I came to realize that I had lucked into a partner who loves me unconditionally, tells me so, and — most of the time — gives me plenty of room. I'm guilty of sometimes taking him for granted, but I do it far less than I did before.

I'm now heading toward 70 and, as I reply to my OB/GYN's annual question, am sexually active with the same, exclusive, partner I have had for over 35 years. Sex has lost its urgency and drama for me. Its pleasures are reliably available but it is only one of many physical, intellectual, emotional and cultural connections Patrick and I share.

My sons have left the town where we first moved in the interests of their education, but Patrick and I remain. We're old people now, relegated to the periphery of things, watching them negotiate their own issues of love and work. I'm still writing and feel blessed to work in a profession that, in its best incarnations, rakes the muck in search of truth.

I go into the city where I grew up far less these days. When I do, I'm struck by the noise and endless distractions. I see how much easier it was for me to become absorbed by other people's stories rather than in my own when I lived there. Occasionally, when I cross Central Park, I'm struck by the sight of a policeman on a blindered horse and remember asking my mother about those blinders. She said that the thick black material narrowed the horse's field of vision, so that he would not be frightened by the many scary things he might otherwise see. Her explanation made sense and, maybe it gave me the idea of constructing my own blinders as a child. They worked well until they didn't. I'm finally able to take them off and take in the view.

Acknowledgments

Many friends and colleagues read, advised and encouraged me over the fifteen years I worked on this memoir. I thank all of them and apologize if I have inadvertently left anyone out.

I first thank my two companions in excavating the past: two gifted and generous men who wish to guard their privacy. Robbie challenged me to write and to keep on writing this book. He gave freely of his time, his insights, and his empathy. I was fortunate to have met him in adolescence and to count him as a friend more than 50 years later. I was equally lucky to have been referred to Dr. M. in 1980 and to have worked with a psychoanalyst of his integrity, flexibility and psychological insight again from 2001 to 2009.

I discussed parts of this memoir with Veronika Ambros, Leah Baigell, Hana Balaban-Pommier, Elisabeth Benjamin, Mary Bralove, Laura Brant, Karen Braziller, Ira Brenner, Amy Brinn, Marshall Brinn, Dawn Cavrell, Hallie Cohen, Daniel Dayan, Jan Drabek, Anne Edelstein, Liz Edelstein, Darlene Ehrenberg, Susan Erony, Eva Fogelman, Rosalie Gerut, Gloria Greenfield, Philippe Grimbert, Joelle Gunther, Judith Gurewich, David Hajdu, Anna Hájková, Trish Hampl, Jill Harkaway, Larry Harmon, Samantha Haywood, Jean Hearst, John Hearst, Barbara Hendra, Judy Herman, Eva Hoffman, Becky Hunt, Margo Jefferson, Jennifer Josephy, Maribeth Kaptchuk, Anne Karpf, Helena Klímová, Henry Kon, Daniela Lax, Martine Lévy, Eva Lorencová, Ellen MacDonald, Alia Martin, Bill Marx, Hilary Mead, Susan Miller,

Spyros Orfanos, Anna Ornstein, (the late) Paul Ornstein, Gail Merrifield Papp, Sonia Pilcer, Susan Hecker Ray, Sophia Richman, Rachel Rosenblum, Demetria Royals, Rochelle Rubinstein, Jill Scobie, Nava Semel, Connie Shuman, Susannah Sirkin, Maria Sirois, Dawn Skorczewski, Gloria Steinem, Helga Stephenson, Susan Suleiman, Monica Szurmuk, Sherry Turkle, Jean Weiss, Nina Willis, Marie Winn and Linda K. Wertheimer.

A special thank you to my many former classmates at P.S. 87 and Hunter College High School for their memories and suggestions, and to my brothers Tom Epstein and David Epstein for their help.

My deepest thanks go to Helen Fremont, who read, edited and reread every draft of this manuscript over fifteen years, and who never stopped telling me how important it was. She is the midwife of this book.

Finally, I could not have written *The Long Half-Lives of Love and Trauma* without the unwavering love and support of my husband, truly ma *moitié.*

About the Author

Helen Epstein (helenepstein.com) is a veteran arts journalist and author of *Children of the Holocaust*, the first book on intergenerational transmission of trauma; *Where She Came From: A Daughter's Search for Her Mother's History*; and the biography *Joe Papp: An American Life*. She is also the translator of Heda Margolius Kovály's *Under a Cruel Star*. She reviews for the New England cultural website *The Arts Fuse* (artsfuse.org).